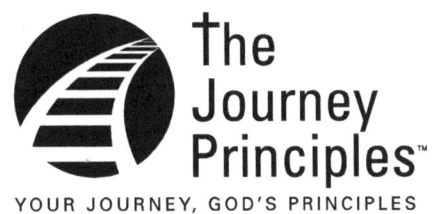

YOUR JOURNEY, GOD'S PRINCIPLES

THE JOURNEY PRINCIPLES
WORKBOOK

10 Week Spiritual Healing Journey

by
Stephen Scoggins
©2014

JOURNEY PRINCIPLES INSTITUTE, INC. PUBLISHING

Copyright © 2014, by Stephen Scoggins

Activities and Graphs by W. Muse Greenwood Copyright © 2014

All rights reserved. No part of this publication may be reproduced, distributed, or transmitted in any form or by any means, including photocopying, recording, or other electronic or mechanical methods, without the prior written permission of the author and publisher, except in the case of brief quotations embodied in critical reviews and certain other noncommercial uses permitted by copyright law. For permission requests, write to the publisher, addressed "Attention: Permissions Coordinator," at the address below.

Journey Principles Institute, Inc. Publishing
423 E. 2nd Street
Clayton, NC 27520
www.stephenscoggins.com
www.journeyprinciples.com

Ordering information: Quantity sales. Special discounts are available on quantity purchases by corporations, associations, and others. For details, contact the publisher at the address above. Orders on-line with various trade bookstores and wholesalers such as Amazon: www.amazon.com.

Printed in the United States of America

The Journey Principles Workbook: 10 Journey Principles / Stephen Scoggins.
ISBN10: 0986278327
ISBN13: 978-0-9862783-2-7
Non-fiction: Motivational, Self-Help, and Spiritual. First Edition

This book is not a substitute for the medical advice of a physician or therapist. The reader should regularly consult a physician in matters relating to his/her health and particularly with respect to any symptoms that may require diagnosis or medical attention. Although the author and publisher have made every effort to ensure that the information in this book was correct at press time, the author and publisher do not assume and hereby disclaim any liability to any party. The intent of the author is only to offer information of a general nature to help you in your quest for spiritual fitness and good health. In the event you use any of the information in this book for yourself, which is your constitutional right, the author and the publisher assume no responsibility for your actions.

Cover Photograph by Kate Kucharzyk
Layout and design by Jeff Lawson, Cowan Graphic Design, Inc.
Curriculum and Book Design by Wendy Muse Greenwood, Inspiration FX,
www.inspirationfx.org

Table of Contents

Stephen Scoggins: From My Heart To Yours — 5

Journey Principle Week 1:
"Understanding Life's Conflicts" — 7

Journey Principle Week 2:
"Growing from Anxiety" — 19

Journey Principle Week 3:
"Isolation is a TRAP!" — 35

Journey Principle Week 4:
"Addiction vs. Sanctification" — 49

Journey Principle Week 5:
"Impatience May Come, but Grace Will Follow" — 65

Journey Principle Week 6:
"Sorrow is an Illusion" — 77

Journey Principle Week 7:
"Pride's Prison" — 89

Journey Principle Week 8:
"Guilt Has Had Us Long Enough" — 101

Journey Principle Week 9:
"Operate in Discernment, Not Deception" — 115

Journey Principle Week 10:
"This Too Shall Pass and What Comes Next Will Be Greater" — 129

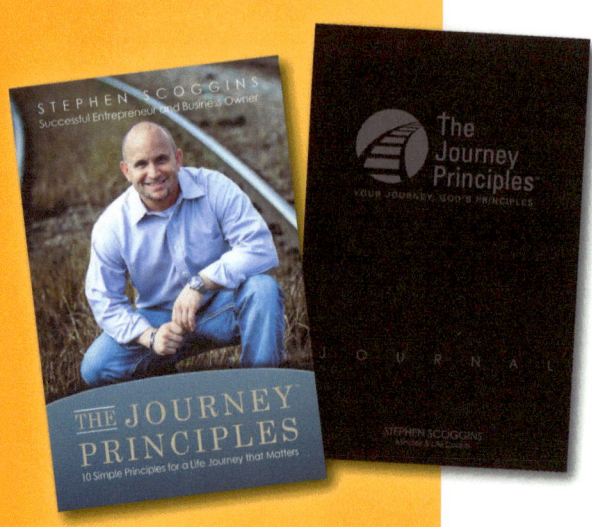

ALSO FROM THE JOURNEY PRINCIPLES™

The Journey Principles
10 Simple Principles for a Life Journey that Matters

Journal
Reflect on your Journey

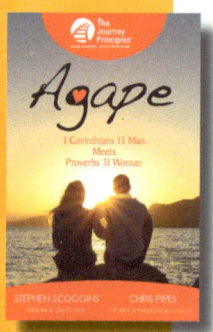

COMING SOON FROM THE JOURNEY PRINCIPLES™

40 Day Walk of Faith
Healing, Hope and Growth
A Daily Devotional

Connect the Dots
A Small Group Study Guide

Build the Owner from Within
12 Essential Principles to Start and Grow your Business

Agape
1 Corinthians 13 Man Meets Proverbs 31 Woman

Heal Grow Go
10 Principles to Overcome a Bullied Life

From my Heart to Yours

The purpose of this book is to encourage and support others during a time of struggle, what we are calling a Journey. The Journey Principles is a combination of the lessons I learned and applied through the grace of God.

This workbook will inspire you to start your Journey, not to give up or give in, but to persevere! It is our hope that you will use our time together wisely. If you are in the middle of a struggle, or have been through challenging times in your life, then this resource is for you!

The truth behind beginning your Journey is knowing that every choice, decision, action, and reaction has a purpose. You have a purpose. If you are willing to learn and grow, your purpose will become clearer with each new step you take.

Consider that the Father wants the best for you. Ask yourself these questions: What is it that God has for you? What must you sacrifice? Who must you become? What must you do? How must you grow?

In this book, each chapter ends with a section for reflective notes where you can write down your growth for the week. These are the realizations that will help you plan your next steps. It is important that you set goals on your Journey and complete this part of the weekly work.

Set your goals, make them measurable.

Give your goals as much detail as you can, tell yourself the steps you need to get there, and put a timetable on them. I encourage you to sit down and pray. As your brother in faith – I pray for your success. To help you on your Journey, I am giving you 10 Principle Prayers for you to access your blessing through purposeful prayer. And brothers and sisters, do not mumble, pour your heart out! Give your fears and struggles over to the Father! I know He wants to hear from you. God the Father is seeking to embrace you. Amen! Your Journey is more important to me than my Journey. My greatest hope by sharing my Journey with you is that you will see how utterly important it is to fulfill yours.

Please don't let pain and sacrifice go by the wayside, please heed my counsel and seek to start, work on, and improve your Journey with renewed vigor and excitement. As always, you can do it, you will do it, and you will change other people's lives because you chose to do it.

I hope these principles will help you make a resolute decision to move forward by letting go of past mistakes and pushing towards your future.

Maybe one day soon we will meet, and you can share how your Journey impacted someone else's life. You are sustained by the prayers of those who blazed a trail before you and the JP Team who supports your new Journey.

As always, it's your Journey, and God's Principles!

In Your Service,
Stephen Scoggins

Week 1

Understanding Life's Conflicts

And the God of all grace, who called you to his eternal glory in Christ, after you have suffered a little while, will himself restore you and make you strong, firm and steadfast.

1 Peter 5:10, NIV

Conflict is the Genesis of Growth.

Obstacle: Conflict
Building Principle: Confidence

Welcome to week one! While I walk with you over the next ten weeks, we will learn, grow, reflect, and pray together. Thank you for allowing The Journey Principles into your life and letting me walk with you on your Journey.

Let's get started!

The Journey Principles was built from many experiences we all face in a lifetime. I have experienced everything from abandonment and rejection to heartbreak and loss many times in my life. I look back now and see how the obstacles I overcame prepared me for a new life of joy and harmony. Without the conflict I experienced, I would never have reached this wonderful place of fulfillment.

Obstacles are not simply something that you go through, around, or over. When you truly confront and overcome an obstacle, it becomes a part of you. It functions as a teaching tool that not only helps you define who you are as an individual, but how you perceive the world and take action in it.

When faced with an obstacle, my faith has been my greatest asset. Through everything I have experienced, God the Father has walked with me every step of the way and He is with each of us on our Journeys. I am grateful for conflict because it draws me closer to Him. Our faith and relationship with God will carry us through the toughest of storms.

Read the story of Noah below and write the lessons you can take away from Noah's demonstration of faith. The Bible tells us that Noah listened to God. What did he hear? He heard God's warning that the world was going to be destroyed. He heard what he had not yet seen.

The LORD then said to Noah, "Go into the ark, you, and your whole family, because I have found you righteous in this generation. Take with you seven pairs of every kind of clean animal, a male and its mate, and one pair of every kind of unclean animal, a male and its mate, and also seven pairs of every kind of bird, male and female, to keep their various kinds alive throughout the earth. Seven days from now I will send rain on the earth for forty days and forty nights, and I will wipe from the face of the earth every living creature I have made."

Genesis 7:1-4

What insight did you gain from Noah's story? Reflect on how can you apply the lessons from this story to your life.

TAKE COURAGE IN CONFLICT
GOD IS GREATER THAN YOUR FEAR

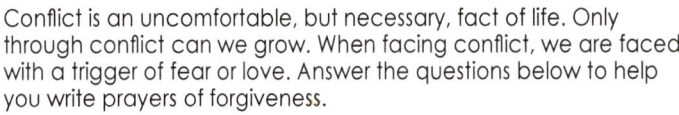

"There is no fear in love. But perfect love drives out fear..."

1 John 4:18, NIV

Conflict is an uncomfortable, but necessary, fact of life. Only through conflict can we grow. When facing conflict, we are faced with a trigger of fear or love. Answer the questions below to help you write prayers of forgiveness.

How would you define a Taker?

_____

_____

_____

How would you describe a Giver?

_____

_____

_____

This is a great start! You may also have a good understanding of Takers and Givers from "The Journey Principles," and let me expand on your definitions of Givers and Takers.

Takers are the kind of people who push forward to fulfill their own desires and life with a self-serving mentality. Both of my parents were once Takers. They were so focused on themselves that they were often oblivious to the impact on my brother and me. As a result, my household was frequently in a state of tension and conflict. The book of Proverbs mentions this kind of conflict, stating: "An unfriendly person pursues selfish ends and against all sound judgment starts quarrels" (Proverbs 18:1, NIV).

The Bible instructs us to be Givers, to "do nothing out of selfish ambition or vain conceit. Rather, in humility value others above yourselves" (Philippians 2:3, NLT). We know that without Christ, being a Giver leaves us feeling overwhelmed. In times of conflict, we must rely on Christ because we can't do it alone!

So when difficulties arise with the people around you, remember to be the Giver and rely on the Lord because He will make sure you're never left feeling empty.

Now let's dive deeper. By understanding the motivating factors of both Givers and Takers, we can recognize when there may be an imbalance in our relationships. Reflect on the questions below and bring your responses to mind when you find yourself confronted with conflict.

Week 1: Understanding Life's Conflicts

Why would fear drive Takers?

_____
_____
_____

Why would love drive Givers?

_____
_____
_____

We are not permanently stuck as Givers or Takers, but there is some give and take in each relationship. Look at the give and take in your relationships. On your first step in this amazing journey, let's see how giving and taking can help you grow.

For the following table, pick three major relationships: How are you a Giver or Taker in each? Prayerfully examine your relationships and acknowledge where God has blessed you and where God can grace you with growth. Through this examination, your relationships will become healthier. Just as Jesus said, "For where two or three gather in my name, there am I with them" (Matthew 18:20, NIV). These healthy relationships will fortify your gratitude and worship.

Relationship	How I Take	How I Give

How can you be more of a Giver and less of a Taker in these relationships?

_____
_____

When is being a Taker healthy in relationships?

_____
_____

Now that you have taken the time to reflect on how you give and take in your relationships, rejoice in knowing that you have taken the first step in our Journey together. You now know a few areas in your relationships that you can give more and some that you can afford to take more. Remember, the key to this lesson is a balance between giving and taking. You will find the balance through God Almighty.

CHANGING THE MEANING

You have just taken a job at a dictionary company. You are responsible for editing a new edition. The only problem is that some of the computers crashed, wiping out various definitions. You have decided to wing it and make up definitions for the words of which you don't know the meaning.

For the following words, write a definition that reflects how each word can make you stronger and help you on your Journey.

The Journey Principles talks about using adversity as a tool to build a better life. Here is your chance to practice and help change your relationships with these words. It will also help you to worship God with a learning heart. By changing these words from a negative to a positive point of view, you will change your relationship with them and build a new story around them. The importance is to build GRATITUDE for how they will sustain you.

Humiliation

_____

_____

_____

Conflict

_____

_____

_____

Unsupported

_____

_____

_____

Journey Principle 1:
"Understanding Life's Conflicts"

In The Journey Principles, I shared my story with you about cleaning a cat box and I felt like I was Jacob wrestling with God. I also share the discernment God shared with me at that moment. Over the next ten weeks, we will read the story of Jacob together and apply these lessons in our lives.

Read the story of Jacob in Genesis 32:1-33:20. Throughout this workbook, I will ask you to look at Jacob's story and find areas in your life where you may have experienced similar emotions or concerns. Take the time to sit back and reflect on those times.

JACOB PREPARES TO MEET ESAU

Jacob went on his way, and the angels of God met him. And when Jacob saw them he said, "This is God's camp!" So he called the name of that place Mahanaim.

And Jacob sent messengers before him to Esau his brother in the land of Seir, the country of Edom, instructing them, "Thus you shall say to my lord Esau: Thus says your servant Jacob, 'I have sojourned with Laban and stayed until now. I have oxen, donkeys, flocks, male servants, and female servants. I have sent to tell my lord, in order that I may find favor in your sight.'"

And the messengers returned to Jacob, saying, "We came to your brother Esau, and he is coming to meet you, and there are four hundred men with him."

Genesis 32: 1-6, ESV

In this section, Jacob was afraid his brother would not forgive him for stealing his birthright. He wanted to reunite with his brother Esau, yet he was sure his sin against his brother was too great to be forgiven.

After you have taken the time to reflect on a time when you felt your trespass was too great to be absolved, say a prayer of praise for the opportunity to grow and learn from that situaton. I challenge you to go one step further and donate something to an organization. This doesn't need to be anything big or extravagant, it can be as simple as volunteering two hours of your time. Pour your heart out to God and let Him know you are grateful.

SEARCHING THE SCRIPTURE FROM WITHIN

Now is the time to take God's Word into your hands and search for the passages that will guide you through your Journey and strengthen your prayer. In the paragraphs that follow, let His Word flow through you and speak to your Journey. By taking the time to review and record His holy Word, you will grow a greater awareness of His awesome power in your life.

1. Don't be afraid of conflict. Too many of us become agitated when we encounter conflict or disagreement out of concern and fear. You need to approach conflict calmly. Consider conflict as a way of learning to see things more clearly. Seek a passage where knowledge was gained from conflict and reflect how you can relate your conflicts to this story to gain understanding.

Scripture:

_____

_____

2. Abandon the concept of winning and losing when faced with conflict. Instead, adopt a strategy of resolution. Think of redirecting the energy toward a common target. Rather than confrontation, you can work together in collaboration to find a solution that suits both sides. Search for a passage to guide you through a conflict in your life.

Scripture:

_____

_____

3. Avoid negative or confrontational language. Try using positive language that disarms rather than confronts, like, "I can see your point, and here is where I'm coming from..." or "I understand your position, and..." Look to Proverbs for strength in knowing that soft words turn away wrath.

Scripture:

_____

_____

4. Talk through the situation with a neutral party to gain perspective and clarity. It is always helpful to get a problem out in the open. People you trust and who understand your frame of reference can provide valuable input. They can help you better understand what you are going through and tell you, for better or worse, whether they think you have properly judged or handled the situation. Look at the passage in the case of two mothers brought before King Solomon in Kings 3: 16-28 for inspiration on how God uses the wisdom of a third party to find the truth.

Scripture:

_____

_____

Week 1: Understanding Life's Conflicts

5. Sometimes you have to clear your mind. Find something to distract you from the conflict. Distance yourself from the problem. Time allows you to reevaluate your position and maybe even come back with a fresh perspective of how to resolve that nagging conflict. Spend some time in the Word of God. Write down the passage that speaks to you and provides you with new insight into your conflict.

Scripture:

_____

_____

QUESTIONS TO MOVE YOU FORWARD
WRITE YOUR ANSWERS ON THE LINES BELOW THE QUESTIONS

God gave us the gift of choice. Learning to ask yourself the right questions is something you have to practice. When we begin to develop this skill, that is when we can truly move forward in both our relationship with Him and in taking the next steps on our Journey.

Name one conflict in your life right now.

_____

_____

Now ask yourself: "What is one thing I can do right now to stop this conflict in my life?"

_____

_____

List five things that make you smile, feel good, or feel safe.

_____

_____

_____

_____

_____

Choose which days you will do one of the things from your "Things That Make Me Smile" list to feel good that day.

_____

_____

Week 1: Understanding Life's Conflicts

SETTING YOUR PATH FOR GROWTH

"If you aim at nothing, you will hit it every time."

Zig Ziglar

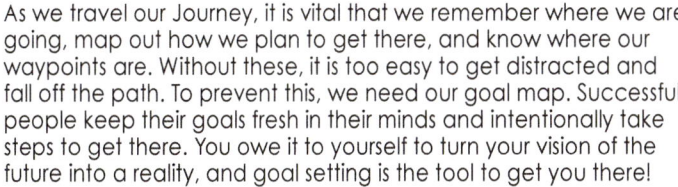

As we travel our Journey, it is vital that we remember where we are going, map out how we plan to get there, and know where our waypoints are. Without these, it is too easy to get distracted and fall off the path. To prevent this, we need our goal map. Successful people keep their goals fresh in their minds and intentionally take steps to get there. You owe it to yourself to turn your vision of the future into a reality, and goal setting is the tool to get you there!

Goals are multi-faceted. For our purposes, each week will focus on goals that reflect the principle we are studying for the week. During these ten weeks and after, make sure that these goals are for YOU! Pray to God for guidance when you set your goals so they may match the path He has carved out for you.

As this is your first goal setting session, start big! What are five significant goals you want to achieve over your lifetime? Brainstorm below to find your starting point.

_____

_____

_____

_____

_____

DISCERNMENT THROUGH GRACE

I hope you have been able to glean that we all have struggles, obstacles and areas to grow. Growth is a Journey. There will be many stops along that Journey, some will be positive and some will be more of a "work in progress."

It's important for us to know ourselves as completely as possible to be ready for the next proverbial step in life's Journey. Have you ever heard the phrase: New Levels have New Devils? Each growth spurt will result in new obstacles, as well as new blessings.

Please ask yourself: Are you a Giver or a Taker? Do you pour into someone's life or do you detract from it? More importantly, ask yourself WHY this is the case.

I have clearly declared that Christ is my Messiah; it is through this proclamation that He has opened both my heart and mind. I can see Him now and I accept Him as The Ultimate Giver. I can truly understand the importance of giving and I understand the Taker is in great need of healing by The Ultimate Giver. I have been both a Giver and a Taker. My Journey has taught me that it is truly more rewarding to give than it is to receive.

Now that you are nearing the end of your first week in The Journey Principles, take the time to reflect on conflict and how your perception has shifted. Write your discernment (spiritual direction and understanding,) of what it means to meet conflict on your Journey. This reflection will be a mile marker as you continue down your path of applying prayer and praise to your healing.

_____

_____

_____

_____

_____

APPLYING THIS PRINCIPLE THROUGH PRAYER

Father in Heaven, please show me guidance, wisdom, and understanding. Please reveal to me the purpose behind the conflicts of my life and how they are meant to build Your kingdom and purpose for my life. Please allow me the grace to see the pain points in my life and Your handprints on them. Prepare my path of healing. In Jesus' name, Amen.

Stephen Scoggins

WRITE YOUR PRAYER

It is through our prayer in God that we are safe in God's love. In His love, we have the space to truly begin our healing. Take a moment, perhaps in a quiet space of your home, and reflect on what you have learned this week. Whether this prayer is for you and your healing or for a loved one, put pen to paper and trust in God's healing power. In the weeks to come, notice how God works in His power to heal all things.

In our first week, we have taken the time to understand how embracing conflict can give us the courage to confront our obstacles. Write a prayer to praise God for the obstacles He has placed in your life. Although the purpose is not always clear, each obstacle that we confront and overcome leads us closer to the person we are meant to be. This prayer will be a reminder that God never gives us more than we can handle.

_____

_____

_____

_____

_____

DRAW YOUR JOURNEY

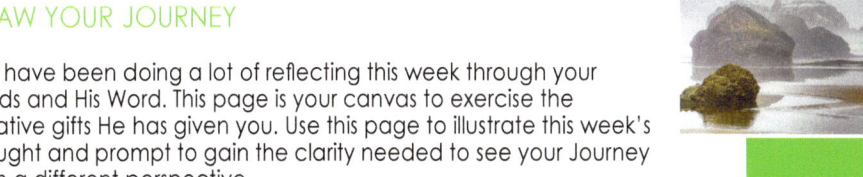

You have been doing a lot of reflecting this week through your words and His Word. This page is your canvas to exercise the creative gifts He has given you. Use this page to illustrate this week's thought and prompt to gain the clarity needed to see your Journey from a different perspective.

Rejoice in your weaknesses, for it is through God that we are made strong. What obstacles has He used in your life to allow you to experience His grace and mercy? Draw a picture of you tearing down this obstacle and accepting conflict as a positive force, as we cannot grow without overcoming adversity. Let your picture be an inspiration to you as you take the first steps on your Journey.

Week 1: Understanding Life's Conflicts

BUILDING PRINCIPLES

Congratulations!

You are well on your way to healing, understanding, and building a stronger relationship with God the Father.

Every step you take on your Journey, you are tearing down the walls that stand in your way. As you take these walls apart, use the blocks to build your foundation for success. This will be your guide as you intentionally shape the foundation for your success.

WEEK 1 BUILDING PRINCIPLE: CONFIDENCE

This week, we are building your foundation for confidence. Find a space to reflect on the lessons from the week and record the messages that have spoken to you about how confidence can shape your Journey. Praise God for the gift of confidence and pray for Him to build yours so that you may have the tool you need to travel your Journey with your head held high, shoulders back, and eyes forward.

_____
_____
_____
_____
_____
_____
_____
_____
_____

"There is no fear in love. But perfect love drives out fear, because fear has to do with punishment. The one who fears is not made perfect in love."

1 John 4:18, NIV

Week 2

Growing from Anxiety

But you, brothers and sisters, are not in darkness so that this day should surprise you like a thief. You are all children of the light and children of the day. We do not belong to the night or to the darkness. So then, let us not be like others, who are asleep, but let us be awake and sober.

1 Thessalonians 5:4-6, NIV

Have faith in uncertainty. God is in control.

Obstacle: Anxiety
Building Principle: Faith

Life is peppered with risks and uncertainty. Personally, I have been through many seasons of anxiety. Like many of you, my brothers and sisters, I have tossed and turned at night because I didn't know what path I should be taking. There were times when I felt empty, used up, and let down by life. I couldn't see His Grand Plan for me when I was battling depression, fear, and anxiety. Only when I was so worn out that I was forced to put my fears at His feet did I find peace. In this moment, I knew that I had to rely on my faith in Christ.

To strengthen our faith, we must build on our ability to speak openly and freely with God. This starts with prayer! Prayer is a beautiful practice where we can speak directly to our Father who loves us. God is the One who will always have a shoulder for us to lean on and a patient ear, open to every worry we have. What's better than that? I'll tell you! The cherry on top of this promise is that He knows what your path will be. He goes before us always. With this knowledge, we can let go of our worries and give them over to Him.

You see, prayer eases those uneasy feelings about the things that may or may not happen. You will face obstacles, but each obstacle is an opportunity to grow closer to God and cultivate a more resilient faith. When the "what ifs" of life cause anxiety, we learn to have faith and act on our trust in God.

While sharing Journey Principle 2, I review a few words related to anxiety and explain the differences in their meaning, their causes, and how they affect us. Here's how I see it:

ANXIETY: Anxiety is our chemical and emotional response to things we do not yet understand or situations where we don't have enough information to know the process or outcome of the next level.

WORRY: Worry is when we give way to anxiety or unease or allow our mind to dwell on difficulty or troubles.

STRESS: Stress is defined as a state of mental or emotional strain or tension resulting from adverse or very demanding circumstances.

This begs the question, "How can I handle my anxious thoughts, worries, and stress?"

Be encouraged! These fearful feelings can be overcome and you can experience peace through times of uncertainty, high demands, and even danger.

Logically, we know that anxiety is related to uncertainty about the present or future. Therefore, there are three approaches to conquering it!

Week 2: Growing from Anxiety

1. For things you can know, but don't know, fill the knowledge gap.

The first step in eliminating uncertainty is through the power of knowledge. If you're anxious about something that may be going wrong, you might be able to learn more about the situation to vanquish the uncertainty.

For example:
- If you're anxious about the doors being unlocked, you can solve it by turning the handles to determine if they are locked or unlocked.
- If you're anxious about getting lost on a trip, you can map out your route or use a GPS to guide you.

2. For things you can't know but you can affect, plan it out.

Business leaders, athletes and chess players all train and develop strategies to counteract an opponent's potential move. By deciding how to handle the unknown, and visualizing how the outcome will be successful, you can get a step closer to understanding and reducing your anxiety.

3. For things you can't know and can't do anything about, let it go and trust in those who care about you. Ultimately give your troubles to God the Father.

Life will throw you curveballs. Unexpected roadblocks come and tragic things can happen. For me, this was when my mom overdosed and barely survived. We must learn to release the burden we can't carry.

Later in this chapter we'll see how faith and trust become tools in your tool belt. We can learn how to manage our thoughts and have courage to face the unknown with confidence and faith. Faith in God enables us to express our fears and desires through prayer. In all its beauty, faith also gives us the gift to celebrate and praise God, even through hard times.

YOU ARE WHAT YOU THINK

On that note, when we understand how to combat anxiety, worry, and stress, we know we have to change our mindsets.

Have you ever heard of self-fulfilling prophesies? The more and more you think about something, the more likely it is that these thoughts will guide your actions. It is important to learn ways you can praise God daily and show your gratitude, which is all part of the praise.

Take a moment and reflect on the following questions to pinpoint what thoughts are constantly on your mind. You will find that by pinpointing these thoughts, you will be able to pray intentionally, worship wholeheartedly, and praise graciously.

1. What do you think about most frequently?

_____
_____

2. What makes you most uncomfortable about the future?

_____
_____

3. If this were to come true, how would you make the conscious choice to turn this into a positive outcome?

_____
_____

4. Read Romans 8:28. Re-write this verse in your own words.

_____
_____

CHANGING THE MEANING

For the following words, write a definition that reflects how each word can make you stronger and help you on your Journey.

The Journey Principles talks about using adversity as a tool to build a better life. Here is your chance to practice and help change your relationships with these words. It will also help you to worship God with a learning heart. By changing these words from a negative to a positive point of view, you will change your relationship with them and build a new story around them. The importance is to build GRATITUDE for how they will sustain you.

Anxiety

_____
_____
_____

Worry

_____
_____
_____

Week 2: Growing from Anxiety

Stress

_____
_____
_____

Journey Principle 2:
"Growing from Anxiety"

Read the story of Jacob in Genesis 32:1-33:20. Throughout this workbook, I will ask you to look at Jacob's story and find areas in your life where you may have experienced similar emotions or concerns. Take the time to sit back and reflect on those times.

JACOB PRAYS

Then Jacob was greatly afraid and distressed. He divided the people who were with him, and the flocks and herds and camels, into two camps, thinking, "If Esau comes to the one camp and attacks it, then the camp that is left will escape."

And Jacob said, "O God of my father Abraham and God of my father Isaac, O Lord who said to me, 'Return to your country and to your kindred, that I may do you good,'

I am not worthy of the least of all the deeds of steadfast love and all the faithfulness that you have shown to your servant, for with only my staff I crossed this Jordan, and now I have become two camps.

Genesis 32: 7-10, ESV

Has there been a time you feared that by telling the truth, you may harm yourself – yet you did it anyway? Reflect on what you learned at that time and how it made you feel.

Say a prayer of praise for the opportunity to be open and honest. When we are honest with ourselves and others, we truly have the freedom to live in His image. This week, seek out someone you love and tell them! Share your heart openly with them and let your love be known. Pour your heart out to God and let Him know you are grateful.

SEARCHING THE SCRIPTURE FROM WITHIN

Now is the time to take God's Word into your hands and search for the passages that will guide you through your Journey and strengthen your prayer. In the paragraphs that follow, let His Word flow through you and speak to your Journey. By taking the time to review and record His holy Word, you will grow a greater awareness of His awesome power in your life.

1. In our lives, there are an infinite amount of unknowns that can cause stress and weaken our faith in ourselves, and at the worst of times, in God. Before beginning this activity, pause to search for the root from which your stress stems. Find a passage where God lifts the stress and worry from the lives of His people and know that He will do the same for you.

Scripture:

_____

_____

2. Our anxiety grows from what we don't know. The beautiful part of not knowing is that He knows all and He has plans designed specifically for each and every one of us. Open your Bible to Proverbs to find what He says about making plans for the future and write down one verse that you will carry with you this week. Find peace when anxiety begins to show itself.

Scripture:

_____

_____

3. Many times, our worries swell inside of us, fed by our negative thoughts and emotions. However, when we speak to Him and express our concerns, He will grant us peace of mind because He cares for us. Find one passage that speaks to this topic to strengthen your faith in the Lord.

Scripture:

_____

_____

4. Do you ever feel like you are standing at the foothills of an insurmountable mountain, tasked with climbing up the steep cliffs? Our obstacles in life can produce these feelings. Yet, with faith, all things are possible. Reflect on a passage, perhaps one you remember hearing or one you are familiar with, where someone was given a task that seemed impossible. How did their faith in God give them the peace they needed to move forward?

Scripture:

_____

_____

Week 2: Growing from Anxiety

QUESTIONS TO MOVE YOU FORWARD
WRITE YOUR ANSWERS ON THE LINES BELOW THE QUESTIONS.

God gave us the gift of choice. Learning to ask yourself the right questions is something you have to practice. When we begin to develop this skill, that is when we can truly move forward in both our relationship with Him and in taking the next steps on our Journey.

What is one prominent worry in your life?

_____

How will you gain knowledge or prepare to accept or affect this event?

_____

_____

List two people you trust to help you through this stress and how you will reach out to them this week.

_____

_____

Write a brief prayer and ask for peace to guide you through this season.

_____

_____

_____

SETTING YOUR PATH FOR GROWTH

"A dream is just a dream. A goal is a dream with a plan and a deadline." – Harvey Mackay

During these ten weeks and after, make sure that these goals are for YOU! Pray to God for guidance when you set your goals to match the path He has carved out for you.

In week one, you listed five goals you want to accomplish. We are going to work together to refine your goals. To accomplish our goals, we need to take each goal, make a plan and set a deadline.

Week 2: Growing from Anxiety

Take one of the goals from week one and map out the steps you need to take to achieve this over the course of a year. For each point, set a reasonable deadline to accomplish the task. By setting the path for your goal, you will know that you are one step closer to reaching your dreams.

_____

_____

_____

_____

_____

_____

Now take your goal map and determine one step you can take THIS week to gain momentum toward accomplishing your goal. Through taking this first step, you will feel a sense of fulfillment and gratitude. Remember, through Him, all things are possible.

_____

_____

_____

FAITH

Faith is our confidence that God will work things out the way He planned. If we really believe that God loves us and that God is in charge of things that happen in the world, then we can let our minds rest and move on with life.

How do we build this confidence in God?

HAVE F.A.I.T.H!

These practices can reinforce your faith in prayer and give clarity in praise.

Fix your eyes on Jesus

I don't mean, "Go look at a statue of Jesus", rather, study and follow the example of Jesus. Most of the stories showing Jesus' example are found in Matthew, Mark, Luke, and John. These books are separate accounts of the life and teachings of Jesus. The authors of these books were people who witnessed Jesus in action. You'll notice that some of the stories are repeated in more than one book.

Let's start with John. Read chapters one through three and reflect on the message and then answer the questions provided below to gain a deeper understanding of faith. You will find peace in your prayer after reading His words.

Week 2: Growing from Anxiety

How did Jesus model prayer and praise? How can you be more aware of Jesus' example?

_____

_____

How did Jesus handle the dangers or difficulties he faced? Did he seem anxious?

_____

_____

Ask God through Prayer

Pray about what worries you and ask for the wisdom to find peace.

Only He knows what has happened, what is happening, and what will happen. When you are anxious and feeling lost, forget about the magic-eight ball! Turn to God and ask Him about your worries. He will ease your mind and bring you peace.

"Do not be anxious about anything, but in every situation, by prayer and petition, with thanksgiving, present your requests to God. And the peace of God, which transcends all understanding, will guard your hearts and your minds in Christ Jesus."

Philippians 4:6-7, NIV

Incorporate Scripture

It's difficult to have faith in anyone you don't know much about. Before you can "take Him at His Word," you need to read the Word, also known as, the Bible.

Here are five ways (think of them like your five fingers) that will help you "get a grip" on the Bible.

1. **Read** the Bible. Approach it like a story or handbook and read it regularly.
2. **Hear** the teachings from preachers, teachers, and experts (podcasts are a great resource) who explain the Bible.
3. **Memorize** it. Having the words in your mind can give you clarity and strength.
4. **Meditate** on it. Think of the stories and words and apply them to your life.
5. **Study** the scriptures. Analyze the meaning and read supporting books.

The Bible is a big book and it can be difficult to know where to start. You may find a reading plan helpful.

Now, any time you start a new routine, it takes 90 days to make it a habit! As Dave Ramsey preaches, "Say it with me, NINETY DAYS!"

How can you incorporate more scripture into your schedule?

_____

Now that's a good start. Here's a tip for you to practice over the remaining eight weeks: When you see a verse mentioned in this workbook, look it up in your Bible. It may take a while to become familiar with the layout, but it's worth exploring along the way. It's also easy to use Google or an App to find passages.

How can you build the habit of remembering scripture when you're anxious?

_____

"When I am afraid, I put my trust in you."

Psalm 56:3, ESV

When you're reading and you see something you like, take a moment to praise God. When you see something you don't understand, take a moment to pray and ask God for understanding.

Track your Journey in a Journal

If you want to learn from your past, it helps to have a written reference. Your Journey will probably have ups and downs. When you can look back, you can praise Him in the high times, and also at the low times. Do you know why? You overcame the low, and you learned from the experience. Throughout the Bible, leaders refer to events in the past where God showed His power and faithfulness. The stories were written, retold, and they were never forgotten.

Reflect on the questions below and use the answers to reveal why recording your Journey will guide you. This reflection will bring you one step closer to praising His name.

Why do you think it's important to write down the stories of your Journey?

_____

_____

How will you track your story: a notepad, a journal, or the margins of your Bible?

_____

_____

Week 2: Growing from Anxiety

Honor One Another

Sharing your Journey and hearing the Journeys of others multiplies encouragement. Whether you are studying this workbook on your own or with a group, use your community to share your experiences. We encourage you to connect with others through The Journey Principles Institute website to share your story or impart lessons your have learned.

Through mentorship, we gain experience through others. In the questions that follow, think of someone who is a mentor in your life and what experiences you have had that could influence others. This will grow your understanding of your Journey and how you can influence others and their Journey.

Who comes to mind when you think of people who inspire you?

_____

_____

_____

What stories from your life could provide encouragement to others?

_____

_____

_____

Applying these five elements of F.A.I.T.H will strengthen you and when the storms of anxiety blow, you will be anchored in this FAITH!

Faith is the key to staying personally centered, but you also need the help of others on your Journey. Faith enables you to be confident in God when life isn't making sense.

However, trust enables you to work with people when you need a hand or a friend.

"Trust is the cement that binds relationships, keeping spouses together, business deals intact and political systems stable. Without trust, marriages fail, voters become apathetic and organizations flounder. Without trust, no person or company can ever hope for excellence. The truth is, trust must be carefully constructed, vigorously nurtured and constantly reinforced."

Frank Sonnenberg

ANXIETY

Anxiety reveals itself in many areas of our lives. It can be in a new relationship or an old one, in a new employment opportunity or leaving behind one. For some, it is the focus of children, and for others, it's a parent with an illness or one who is on their way to

heaven. Remember, anxiety is just our chemical and emotional response to things we do not yet know or don't have enough information to understand the process or see the outcome of the next level.

This workbook came out of the very things that brought anxiety into my Journey. I want to emphasize that once we properly channel our anxiety, this obstacle becomes growth for understanding.

Anxiety comes from that which we don't understand.

Think of the top five anxieties of your life. Got 'em? Hold onto them and release them here:

_____

_____

_____

_____

_____

Don't give them power, but understand that you only need more information and that it may be some time before you properly understand the present information or information to come.

Now that you have written them down, let's decide one-by-one how we will gather factual and non-emotional information about them. Think broadly: What do you know or what can you learn to understand the causes of these challenges?

_____

What parts are unknowable or unpredictable?

_____

How will you seek the answers and understanding?

_____

How will you take steps to rely on faith and trust?

_____

_____

_____

God the Father could easily use facts to show His clear path for our lives, but allows enough uncertainty for us to walk in faith with Him.

Week 2: Growing from Anxiety

APPLYING THIS PRINCIPLE THROUGH PRAYER

Father in Heaven, thank you so much for your grace, power, and mercy. Please deliver me from all things in my life, my relationships and my actions, that bring forth any essence of anxiety! Help me to see that which you have planned for me. Land me sure-footed on the sturdy ground and remove that which causes uneasiness in my life or help me to see the purpose behind its design. All of Heaven and Earth is in Your hands. In Jesus' name, Amen.

Stephen Scoggins

WRITE YOUR PRAYER

What is speaking to your heart this week? Through our study, we know that the God Almighty is stronger than any fear, anxiety, or struggle. Consider a prayer of praise. Thank Him for all He does and continues to do in your life. By giving thanks, we open the door for God to do more in our lives and shape us into the men and women He calls us to be.

_____

_____

_____

_____

_____

DRAW YOUR TESTIMONY

You have been doing a lot of reflecting this week through your words and His Word. This page is your canvas to exercise the creative gifts He has given you. Use this page to illustrate this week's thought and prompt to gain the clarity needed to see your Journey from a different perspective.

Think of two causes of anxiety in your life. For these causes, consider how Scripture, faith, and trust can help combat the anxiety. In the space below, draw how you envision the anxiety disappearing. Next time the anxiety begins to boil up, this picture will provide you with the calm you need to confront the root of your anxiety with confidence.

BUILDING PRINCIPLES

Congratulations!

You are well on your way to healing, understanding, and building a stronger relationship with God the Father.

Every step you take on your Journey, you are tearing down the walls that stand in your way. As you take these walls apart, use the blocks to build your foundation for success. This will be your guide as you intentionally shape the foundation for your success.

WEEK 2 BUILDING PRINCIPLE: FAITH

This week, we focused on combatting anxiety with faith. Take a moment to write about how you will strengthen your faith in God and how you will work to strengthen trust in one of your relationships. Over time, you will build a community of support who will only want to see you succeed. Through this community, you will find that the anxiety will melt away.

_____

_____

_____

_____

_____

_____

_____

_____

_____

"These are truths which can prepare us to respond when crisis and fear come into our lives."

C.S. Lewis

Week 3

Isolation is a TRAP!

As Jesus was walking beside the Sea of Galilee, he saw two brothers, Simon called Peter and his brother Andrew. They were casting a net into the lake, for they were fishermen. "Come, follow me," Jesus said, "and I will send you out to fish for people." At once they left their nets and followed him.

Matthew 4:18-20, NIV

The Journey Principles™
YOUR JOURNEY, GOD'S PRINCIPLES

Accept help from others. God uses people to give life.

Obstacle: Isolation
Building Principle: Family

As we learned from Journey Principle 2, our trust in others is what helps lighten our burden. All too often, we find ourselves falling into the "lone ranger" complex. We want to be independent and do everything on our own.

When we fall prey to this complex, we begin to feel isolated and utterly alone. One of the fastest growing epidemics in our nation is depression. It often goes unseen and undiagnosed, until it manifests itself on a drastic scale. I saw this with my mother when I was at a very young age and have walked that path myself. In our society, I believe there are two main contributors:

1. Our ever-growing desire for individualism

2. The rapid increase in technology

Individualism becomes unhealthy when it pushes away or harms others around you. The further you push your loved ones away, the more isolated and lonely you can feel.

Now, I want to take a moment to touch on social media. We have the gift to stay in touch with friends and family millions of miles away through technology, whether it is Facebook or e-mail. Yet, just as the Israelites hoarded their mana (even when God told them not to,) we know that too much of a good thing can spoil your life.

For this exercise, log in to your social media account you use most frequently and write down how many friends or followers you have: _____

Out of these friends/followers, how many would you call a true friend? _____

By looking at these numbers, consider what it means to have a community. Name three of your true friends and how you will connect with them this week (by giving them a call, meeting with them for a meal, etc.).

_____

_____

"You don't build a business -- you build people – and the people build the business."

Zig Ziglar

When we're hurt, it's natural to withdraw in fear or burn bridges in anger. But when we cut others off, we're really cutting ourselves off. According to Proverbs 18:1 NKJV, "A man who isolates himself seeks his own desire; He rages against all wise judgment."

But God didn't make us that way! You can try to carry the weight by yourself, but it's so much easier when you have the right support group to help you shoulder the load.

When we are born, God gives us a small network: a family. Families are designed to be supportive, enriching and meaningful. When you think of family, your memories may not all be pretty. When I think of my family, I remember arguments during my parents' divorce, feelings of bitterness, and abandonment. I also remember love and encouragement, birthdays and holidays celebrated with at least some members of the family. We can both hurt and heal the people closest to us.

Hurt people- Hurt people!

A dog with its leg crushed in a trap is likely to bite you even if you're trying to set it free. In the same way, when we feel trapped, hurt, or afraid, we tend to lash out at the people around us. Even if we know they mean well.

Think of a time when you overreacted or said something hurtful because you were in pain. How did your action make the other person feel?

_____

_____

Assuming you weren't hurt at the time, how might you have handled the situation differently?

_____

_____

This may be a hard lesson to learn, but don't be discouraged, because the reverse is true too.

Healed people- Heal people!

The first step in developing a healthy support team has nothing to do with choosing the "right" friends. Before you can trust the opinions and feedback from those closest to you, you must know yourself first! Relationships are built on trust and as we explored in the last principle, trust begins with you.

Knowing yourself is not as simple as stating it in a social meme, a socially accepted belief system, or identifying yourself by fundamental ethics. It means acting in accordance with your beliefs, not just occasionally, but consistently. Every day should reflect your beliefs, character, and integrity. This is not to say that these beliefs won't develop over time based on your experiences and learned lessons, but simply be mindful that your reputation is judged by the things you do consistently.

Ultimately, we rub off on each other. This can be a good thing! There is a reason why we are inclined to be generous around Christmas. When we are healthy, happy and at peace, our joy will overflow into others' lives.

We are going to look at both the hurt people and the healed people in your life. The steps you are about to take may be difficult, but take heart in knowing that this will help you make progress toward being a healed person yourself. In God's healing, we can worship and praise His name.

A 3D Family: Relationships

Family has relationships in 3 directions: up, down and sideways. You may have a father or mother (up relationship), brother or sister (sideways relationship), or son or daughter (down relationship). We need relationships in these three directions throughout life. The same 3D theory relates to Patron, Peer, and Protégé. Let's take a look:

Up Relationship: Parent / Patron / Mentor

We need someone to mentor or coach us in life. This is someone you can ask for advice, direction, or support. I recommend having at least one person in your life who is older, or at least wiser and experienced, who can mentor you on your Journey.

It is also good to learn from many teachers, authors or leaders through books, videos, and broadcasts.

Who serves as a mentor or coach for you?

_____

What qualities must someone have for you to accept him or her as a mentor or coach?

_____

Sideways Relationship: Sibling / Peer / Friend

We can go farther when we have a friend or teammate. Look for a friend or ally who can understand what you're facing, can spot when you're getting off track and will be there to help you carry on.

In the chapter on Journey Principle 3, I use the example of Clydesdales (the big horses from the Budweiser commercials) working together. When two Clydesdales harness their strength, together, they can pull double the weight of one on its own. The same principle is true for friendships.

Most athletes have experienced the effect of having a buddy to run or workout with.
In what areas of life do you need a "running buddy"?

_____

In this same area of your life, who can you partner with to encourage one another?

_____

Down Relationship: Child / Protégé / Student

Have you ever lead a hike or been the lead car when driving somewhere the other person was unfamiliar with? This relationship is very similar where you are the leader. When we take on this role, we are emulating Jesus and how He was the benevolent shepherd.

We see our steps more clearly when someone is following us and we learn best when we teach someone else. Adding value to others gives meaning to your Journey.

Name someone who you think you could be a mentor to. How will you propose your mentorship and in what area of their life can you add value?

_____

_____

CHANGING THE MEANING

For the following words, write a definition that reflects how this word/experience in your life makes you stronger and how it aids you on your Journey.

The Journey Principles talks about using adversity as a tool to build a better life. Here is your chance to practice and help you change your relationships with these words. It will also help you to worship God with a learning heart. By changing these words, you will change your relationship with them, build a new story around them, and the importance is to build GRATITUDE for how they will sustain you.

Trap

_____

_____

Isolation

_____

_____

Hurt

_____

_____

_____

Journey Principle 3:
"Isolation is a TRAP!"

Read the story of Jacob in Genesis 32:1-33:20. Throughout this workbook, I will ask you to look at Jacob's story and find areas in your life where you may have experienced similar emotions or concerns. Take the time to sit back and reflect on those times.

JACOB FOLLOWS GOD'S WILL

Please deliver me from the hand of my brother, from the hand of Esau, for I fear him that he may come and attack me, the mothers with the children.

But you said, 'I will surely do you good, and make your offspring as the sand of the sea, which cannot be numbered for multitude.'"

So he stayed there that night, and from what he had with him he took a present for his brother Esau, two hundred female goats and twenty male goats, two hundred ewes and twenty rams, thirty milking camels and their calves, forty cows and ten bulls, twenty female donkeys and ten male donkeys.

These he handed over to his servants, every drove by itself, and said to his servants, "Pass on ahead of me and put a space between drove and drove."

Genesis 32: 11-16, ESV

Recall a time when you were unsure of what God had planned for you. In this time, God was speaking to your heart and revealing His will to you. What was the lesson learned in that moment?

Your brothers and sisters in Christ may also be unsure of the paths God is leading them on. Our role is to guide and encourage them in His plan. Encourage someone this week. Buy a flower and give it to a stranger with a smile. You never know how one small act of kindness can have a ripple effect. Pour your heart out to God and let Him know you are grateful.

SEARCHING THE SCRIPTURE FROM WITHIN

Now is the time to take God's Word into your hands and search for the passages that will guide you through your Journey and strengthen your prayer. In the paragraphs that follow, let His Word flow through you and speak to your Journey. By taking the time to review and record His holy Word, you will grow a greater awareness of His awesome power in your life.

1. When we feel like we are alone, it is the hardest thing to know that we are loved and cared for. Yet we are. We have a community waiting for us to reach out for help when we need it. Find one passage where, through the power of God's community, the goals of many were accomplished. While finding, reading, and recording this passage, relate how your community (even if it is a small community of one or two) can help you on your Journey.

Scripture:

_____

_____

2. Think of one pair of friends in the Bible who lifted one another up. Find a passage resembling this friendship and apply it to your life. Be cognizant of how this friendship keeps you motivated on your Journey.

Scripture:

_____

_____

3. As we travel our Journey, our friendships change with the ebb and flow of time. We go through seasons where we are with the same friend or mentor and others where many come and go. Search for a verse or a Psalm praising His name for walking with us.

Scripture:

_____

_____

4. Have you ever found yourself in the presence of a false friend? At the time, it may have been hard for you to see that this relationship was damaging to you and your Journey. Look at 2 Timothy to see what is said about those who walk in the light of God and what is said about those who have been led astray by sin. Let the Word of God wash over you and absorb the message so that you may recognize a false friend and learn to build a true friendship.

Scripture:

_____

_____

Week 3: Isolation is a TRAP!

QUESTIONS TO MOVE YOU FORWARD
WRITE YOUR ANSWERS ON THE LINES BELOW THE QUESTIONS

God gave us the gift of choice. Learning to ask yourself the right questions is something you have to practice. When we begin to develop this skill, that is when we can truly move forward in both our relationship with Him and in taking the next steps on our Journey.

Recall a season when you were a healed person. How did you heal those around you?

_____

Who is a mentor to you and how have they shaped your Journey? If you are still searching for a mentor, consider where you need guidance on your Journey and how you may reach out to a mentor this week.

_____

_____

How do you think being a patron, partner, and protégé will add value to your Journey?

_____

_____

Write a brief prayer of praise to God for the blessing of family and friendship.

_____

_____

_____

SETTING YOUR PATH FOR GROWTH

"I can do things you cannot, you can do things I cannot; together we can do great things."
Mother Teresa

During these ten weeks and after, make sure that these goals are for YOU! Pray to God for guidance when you set your goals to match the path He has carved out for you.

Last week, we made a goal map for one out of the five goals

Week 3: Isolation is a TRAP!

you set for week one. How did that go? What were you able to accomplish? Write a brief paragraph about how you took the first step. When you journal your experience, you have a point of reference and when you accomplish your goal, you can reflect on the Journey you took to get there.

_____

_____

_____

_____

Do you feel that it is up to you and you alone to accomplish your five goals? I want you to take this thought and cast it aside! As we are studying this week, isolation is a trap and a tricky one at that. We are never alone in life because we have God. He is with us always and He does not want us to pull the load of life on our own, so He has sent you a support team!

Name 3 people who are on your team and jot down ways they will help you accomplish your goals. These are the cheerleaders, the motivators, the relay team, and your champions. If you want, put me down as one! I am here for you.

_____

_____

_____

Week 3: Isolation is a TRAP!

NEW PERSPECTIVE ON KINGDOM-MINDED THINGS

A true starting point begins with where you are standing and the lens you are looking through. Our perception is the greatest key to influencing our lives. Let's seek proper perspective first, and through growth, a fulfilled life of hope and healing will follow.

At times, life can feel like a maze. There are many emotional and psychological benefits to the problem-solving processes. A maze is a task where we have to make decisions about what to do at certain points, in order to continue towards a final goal.

This activity is a great way to practice setting out to achieve something that may appear challenging at first.

Week 3: Isolation is a TRAP!

APPLYING THIS PRINCIPLE THROUGH PRAYER

Oh, Heavenly Father, please install a hedge of protection over me and give your angels charge of me, keeping me from the evil one. I know he wants to isolate me in aloneness or in unhealthy relationships. Father, please guide me towards life-giving relationships, relationships that are full of your love, mercy, and grace. Create in me a life-giving spirit so I may guide others to you and your purpose for them. In Jesus' name, Amen.

Stephen Scoggins

WRITE YOUR PRAYER

Take a moment to reflect on your discernment from the week. Write a prayer asking God to send the right teacher, mentor and patron into your life. Pray for the time to gain understanding, clarity, and vision of whom God created you to be today. With a shepherd in your life, you will develop into a stronger, healthier, and deeply spiritual man or woman. Let this teacher be the lighthouse as you walk your Journey.

_____

_____

_____

_____

_____

_____

Week 3: Isolation is a TRAP!

DRAW YOUR JOURNEY

You have been doing a lot of reflecting this week through your words and His Word. This page is your canvas to exercise the creative gifts He has given you. Use this page to illustrate this week's thought and prompt to gain the clarity needed to see your Journey from a different perspective.

Fold this page in half, go ahead, it's okay, I'm not going to be offended! On the left side of the chart, the side farthest from the spine of the book, draw yourself as you are now. On the right-hand side, draw someone who you respect as a mentor, patron, or teacher. By looking at these interpretations side-by-side, you will see the attributes you want to incorporate along your Journey.

Week 3: Isolation is a TRAP!

BUILDING PRINCIPLES

Congratulations!

You are well on your way to healing, understanding, and building a stronger relationship with God the Father.

Every step you take on your Journey, you are tearing down the walls that stand in your way. As you take these walls apart, use the blocks to build your foundation for success. This will be your guide as you intentionally shape the foundation for your success.

WEEK 3 BUILDING PRINCIPLE: FAMILY

This week, we looked at isolation and learned we can overcome this through the bonds of family. Family is not limited to blood bonds; it includes friends, mentors, etc. and those who truly have your best interests at heart. Reflect on who these people are in your life and how you can thank them along your Journey. These will be your champions as you continue your walk.

_____

_____

_____

_____

_____

_____

_____

_____

_____

"But seek ye first the kingdom of God, and his righteousness; and all these things shall be added unto you."

Matthew 6:33, KJV

Week 4

Addiction vs. Sanctification

Not that I have already obtained all this, or have already arrived at my goal, but I press on to take hold of that for which Christ Jesus took hold of me. Brothers and sisters, I do not consider myself yet to have taken hold of it. But one thing I do: Forgetting what is behind and straining toward what is ahead, I press on toward the goal to win the prize for which God has called me heavenward in Christ Jesus.

Philippians 3:12-14, NIV

See your brokenness. God heals broken people.

Obstacle: Addiction
Building Principle: Sanctification

This chapter is about BEING REAL with yourself, and seeing the busted up parts of your life. But it's not just about admitting we need help, it's about the hope that real change can happen in your life and new life can grow in areas you see as dead. Radical change and finding freedom from life-wrecking habits is not usually quick or easy; though God sometimes heals or changes people in dramatic and miraculous ways. This chapter is not simply about having faith or praying for a sudden miracle. Instead, it's about having faith while and praying and working towards a miracle.

Bad habits start with the thought of "just this once" and then it becomes consistent until it develops into a necessity. The problem is, most of the things we get hooked on can't make us happy. C.S. Lewis said in *Mere Christianity*, "All that we call human history: money, poverty, ambition, war, prostitution, classes, empires, slavery, [is] the long, terrible story of man trying to find something other than God which will make him happy."

Like ruts, habits are hard to get out of and it seems there's mud everywhere. The process of breaking free goes through several stages.

1. Facing the facts
2. Committing to change
3. Finding hope and strength in God
4. Rebuilding belief in self
5. Getting help
6. Helping others

Sin and addiction are like slavery and bondage.

Addiction doesn't equal sin, but they have similar traits and sometimes overlap. Coping with addiction may cause you to develop behaviors that become necessary, harmful, compulsive, or irrational.

Perhaps there is a substance, behavior, or persistent thought you can't shake and you feel powerless to resist. We must keep this in mind to stay free from bondage and idolatry (the love or worship of anything other than God Himself). In Journey Principle 3, we talked about how too much of a good thing, even a gift from God, can cause spoil and ruin. God freed us from our sin by sending His only Son to die on the cross so that we could be presented pure and blameless when we return home.

You may be saying, "Stephen, there are things in my life that I enjoy doing, but I wouldn't say that I'm addicted." I pray that you are correct, but I believe that most people can find at least one addiction in their life if they look closely enough.

Let's look at a general breakdown of common types of addictions. In each section, identify some addictions that may apply in your life:

> **Chemical:** Drugs, alcohol, pills, cigarettes, coffee, diet soda, energy drinks

> **Psychological:** Shopping, spending, pornography, food, eating disorders, gambling, video games, TV, social media, work

> **Abstract:** Lying, success, sex, approval, negativity, gossip

The amazing thing is, people have overcome dependence from each of these addictions. I promise that you will want the life God has for you; it is far better than what you can possibly imagine for yourself and far more satisfying than any earthly pleasure.

We need to identify what these things are in our lives. In my Journey, I experienced an emotional and physical addiction to a relationship.

God gave us a body and free will, so we need to watch for things that we crave or that attack us physically.

God, created our emotional fortitude to be built over time, so what is preventing us from being emotionally healthy?

I'm about to ask you to take a hard look in the mirror. The questions I am going to ask you are to help you examine what may be an addiction for you. Once you identify the addiction, you can take ownership to move forward and pray for guidance to desire what God wants for you.

Week 4: Addiction vs. Sanctification

List 3 things that seem to pull you away from being totally "healthy."

1. _____
2. _____
3. _____

What gives you comfort?

_____
_____

What makes you sad or angry if you miss or fail to participate in it?

_____
_____

What do you do daily that started as a one-time indulgence?

_____
_____

This is what I know: you can survive an enslaving habit for a while, but to be fully alive, you'll need to release, change, and grow.

I hope by now we are starting to see that addictions pose a serious threat by making us settle for anything less than what God has planned for us to be or become.

My last question in this segment for you may be the most difficult. What is preventing your spiritual health? Most times we only need to realize that we have fallen short and need Christ's help to overcome.

_____
_____
_____
_____

Remember when we discussed how hurt people hurt people and it works the opposite way too? The same is true for addiction. The opposite of addiction is sanctification.

Week 4: Addiction vs. Sanctification

If Addiction is:

Involuntary **slavery**
to a **mindless** substance or **life-draining** behavior,
that makes us **less and less ourselves**.

Sanctification is the Opposite:

Voluntary **service**
to a **personal** and **life-giving** God
who makes us **more and more ourselves**.

Sanctification is the process of becoming freer, more whole, and more yourself in God. Sanctified is a fancy word to say "free in God." As God sanctifies you, He shapes you more and more into the image of Christ so that you become more like Jesus in your thoughts, desires, actions and words.

CASE STUDY: A LOOK AT AA

One organization has made a huge impact on helping people in recovery from life-destroying alcoholism. Alcoholics Anonymous (AA) has used a 12 Step program with a group setting, mentors, and social accountability to change countless lives. You may have had a friend or relative go through the program, or it might be something you've seen first hand. The process is time-consuming but effective. Members regularly attend group meetings, report on recent events or progress, celebrate victories and develop friendships. Members are also connected to a "sponsor" or mentor who coaches them through the process. Here are the 12 Steps outlined in "The Big Book":

THE TWELVE STEPS OF ALCOHOLICS ANONYMOUS

1. We admitted we were powerless over alcohol – that our lives had become unmanageable.
2. Came to believe that a Power greater than ourselves could restore us to sanity.
3. Made a decision to turn our will and our lives over to the care of God as we understood Him.
4. Made a searching and fearless moral inventory of ourselves.
5. Admitted to God, to ourselves, and to another human being the exact nature of our wrongs.
6. Were entirely ready to have God remove all these defects of character.
7. Humbly asked Him to remove our shortcomings.
8. Made a list of all persons we had harmed, and became willing to make amends to them all.
9. Made direct amends to such people wherever possible, except when to do so would injure them or others.
10. Continued to take personal inventory and when we were wrong promptly admitted it.
11. Sought through prayer and meditation to improve our conscious contact with God, as we understood Him, praying only for knowledge of His will for us and the power to carry that out.
12. Having had a spiritual awakening as the result of these Steps, we tried to carry this message to alcoholics and to practice these principles in all our affairs.

Copyright © 1952, 1953, 1981 by Alcoholics Anonymous Publishing (now known as Alcoholics Anonymous World Services, Inc.) All rights reserved.

STUDY THE CASE

What stands out to you about the 12 Steps?

_____

_____

Why do you think this organization and their process have been so effective?

_____

_____

What correlation do you see between the 12 steps and what we have learned so far? How can this bring victory on your Journey?

_____

_____

Week 4: Addiction vs. Sanctification

What is it about your habit or addiction that makes it so difficult to break?

_____

_____

How does it affect our praise when we yield our will to God's Power?

_____

_____

REBUILDING YOUR IDENTITY AND SELF-WORTH

The Flea Circus

Life can be like a flea circus. Zig Ziglar used to tell a story that I fell in love with. It was all about how fleas are trained for the circus. You see, when a flea is in the open world, with no limits, they can jump as high as the eyes can see. A flea gets into the jar and the lid is placed on the top. The flea begins to jump, bumping its head, again, again and again; until finally it begins to jump a little less, a little less and a little less. Pretty soon, the flea is only jumping high enough to touch the lid. It's as if the flea begins to give up on life, losing a little more of its self-worth each day, with each jump.

What lids have you placed over your head and how do they limit you?

_____

_____

We are a bit like the flea. When we are young, we think can do anything! There is no shortage of time and no focus on failures. We then grow and face life in all its glory and pain with "job failures," relationships, character flaws, family, friends, and much more.

How can you lift those lids?

_____

_____

The sad part is, if you let the flea out of the jar, it will keep jumping to the height of the lid and no further. It's as if the flea has forgotten what it's capable of.

Our self-worth falls apart in much of the same way. The more we bump into the ceiling of life, the more we begin to lose our hope and motivation. This was the case in my life because of certain lids I placed over my head. I began to stop jumping, even after I jumped so high. But unlike the flea, when my lid was removed, my fall allowed me to reset and learn about humility and appreciate blessings.

Reflect on your childhood dreams. What was one dream you left behind because you were told or told yourself, that you were reaching too high?

_____

_____

I want you to pause and think. It takes honest thought and reflection for the ideas to make sense, to stick in your mind, and shape your view of yourself. This activity can help you regain confidence in prayer and joy in praise.

Revisit the possibility of achieving this dream. Write your first step to making this come true.

_____

_____

CHANGING THE MEANING

For the following words, write a definition that reflects how each word can make you stronger and help you on your Journey.

The Journey Principles talks about using adversity as a tool to build a better life. Here is your chance to practice and help change your relationships with these words. It will also help you to worship God with a learning heart. By changing these words from a negative to a positive point of view, you will change your relationship with them and build a new story around them. The importance is to build GRATITUDE for how they will sustain you.

Addiction

_____

_____

_____

Idolatry

_____

_____

_____

Hurt

_____

_____

_____

Journey Principle 4:
"Addiction vs. Sanctification"

Read the story of Jacob in Genesis 32:1-33:20. Throughout this workbook, I will ask you to look at Jacob's story and find areas in your life where you may have experienced similar emotions or concerns. Take the time to sit back and reflect on those times.

JACOB WRESTLES

He instructed the first, "When Esau my brother meets you and asks you, 'To whom do you belong? Where are you going? And whose are these ahead of you?' then you shall say, 'They belong to your servant Jacob. They are a present sent to my lord Esau.

And moreover, he is behind us.'" He likewise instructed the second and the third and all who followed the droves, "You shall say the same thing to Esau when you find him, and you shall say, 'Moreover, your servant Jacob is behind us.'

For he thought, "I may appease him with the present that goes ahead of me, and afterward I shall see his face. Perhaps he will accept me." So the present passed on ahead of him, and he himself stayed that night in the camp.

Genesis 32: 17-21, ESV

When have you been afraid to meet the face of someone you wronged? Reflect on this moment and consider how you approached the situation. How were you able to meet the gaze of this person? Recall what you learned in this moment and hold onto this lesson as you continue your Journey.

In moments of struggle and doubt, give something of yourself. Over the next five days, consider and then act on how your actions can improve the lives of others by giving words of advice, kindness, and encouragement. Pour your heart out to God and let Him know you are grateful.

MATTHEW HENRY'S CONCISE COMMENTARY ON 1 CORINTHIANS 6:12-20

Matthew Henry was a scholar, theologian, and preacher of the 18th Century. Best known for his six-volume "Exposition of the Old and New Testaments" and the "Complete Commentary," Henry provides an extensive study of each Bible verse. Henry's works are practical and intended for devotional use.

Below, we will look at 1 Corinthians 6:12. Even five centuries later, Henry's insight is applicable in our world today. Read the passage and commentary with an open mind and heart.

"All things are lawful unto me, but all things are not expedient: all things are lawful for me, but I will not be brought under the power of any."

1 Corinthians 6:12, KJV

Some among the Corinthians seem to have been ready to say, "all things are lawful for me". This is the dangerous conceit St. Paul opposes. There is a liberty wherewith Christ has made us free, in which we must stand fast. But surely a Christian would never put himself into the power of any bodily appetite. The body is for the Lord; is to be an instrument of righteousness to holiness, therefore is never to be made an instrument of sin. It is an honor to the body, that Jesus Christ was raised from the dead; and it will be an honor to our bodies, that they will be raised. The hope of a resurrection to glory, should keep Christians from dishonoring their bodies by fleshly lusts. And if the soul be united to Christ by faith, the whole man is become a member of his spiritual body. Other vices may be conquered in fight; that here cautioned against, only by flight. And vast multitudes are cut off by this vice in its various forms and consequences. Its effects fall not only directly upon the body, but often upon the mind. Our bodies have been redeemed from deserved condemnation and hopeless slavery by the atoning sacrifice of Christ. We are to be clean, as vessels fitted for our Master's use. Being united to Christ as one spirit, and bought with a price of unspeakable value, the believer should consider himself as wholly the Lord's, by the strongest ties. May we make it our business, to the latest day and hour of our lives, to glorify God with our bodies, and with our spirits which are his.

SEARCHING THE SCRIPTURE FROM WITHIN

Now is the time to take God's Word into your hands and search for the passages that will guide you through your Journey and strengthen your prayer. In the paragraphs that follow, let His Word flow through you and speak to your Journey. By taking the time to review and record His holy Word, you will grow a greater awareness of His awesome power in your life.

1. Our addictions and temptations are different and unique to our own Journey. Yet, the struggle to resist and come back to the path God mapped for us is the same. Leaf through the Bible and find verses where God promises that He will deliver you from temptation. Be encouraged in knowing through prayer and praise, He will help you through your struggles.

Scripture:

_____

_____

2. Search your heart to find what you struggle to live without. Is this preventing you from growing closer to Him? Spend some time in the Word to find strength and listen to God for the steps you can take to free yourself from addiction.

Scripture:

_____

_____

3. When we accept Christ into our hearts and turn our lives back over to Him, we are washed clean of our sin by the blood He spilled on the cross. Amen! Through His glory and unto His will, we are free from the evils that tempt us towards sin and we are guided by His light and grace on our Journey! What verse speaks to your heart and allows you to see yourself as a FREE child of God? When temptation begins whispering into your ear, speak this verse loud and clear and know He is there to carry you on the straight path.

Scripture:

_____

_____

4. God forgives. How beautiful is that? He knows that we are imperfect, though made in His image and through His love, we are made new. Find scripture that gives you the inspiration and strength to leave the old you who struggles behind and the will to be made new in His likeness.

Scripture:

_____

_____

QUESTIONS TO MOVE YOU FORWARD
WRITE YOUR ANSWERS ON THE LINES BELOW THE QUESTIONS

God gave us the gift of choice. Learning to ask yourself the right questions is something you have to practice. When we begin to develop this skill, that is when we can truly move forward in both our relationship with Him and in taking the next steps on our Journey.

What are three steps you will take to break free from an addiction in your life?

1. _____

2. _____

3. _____

Week 4: Addiction vs. Sanctification

How will you ask God for sanctification?

_____

_____

Spread the good news. Who will you teach about lifting limitations?

_____

_____

Write a brief prayer of praise to God for the blessing of dreaming big.

_____

_____

_____

SETTING YOUR PATH FOR GROWTH

"Discipline is the bridge between goals and accomplishment."

Jim Rohn

During these ten weeks and after, make sure that these goals are for YOU! Pray to God for guidance when you set your goals to match the path He has carved out for you.

This week, we are going to shift gears. In Journey Principle 4, we are looking at how to overcome addiction with sanctification. Bring to mind one addiction you are struggling with. Your addiction may not be something that comes to mind readily; it may be as subtle as spending too much time on Facebook or working long hours.

Now that you have it in your mind, what are three goals you can set to step away from this addiction and closer toward your relationship with God?

_____

_____

_____

Our quote for goal setting this week has us take a close look at discipline. Have you ever started something that you thought would be the difference between where you were and where you wanted to be? I think we all experience this at one point or another. Recall a time when you maintained discipline. How will you stay disciplined to stay on the path you mapped out last week?

_____

_____

_____

Make the promise to yourself this week to stay disciplined and take another step toward your goal. You can accomplish your dreams if you choose to. I believe in you.

APPLYING THIS PRINCIPLE THROUGH PRAYER

My Father, who is in Heaven, holy is Your name. Please show me the areas in my life that take me away from You and the addictions that are in front of my relationship with You. Please help me break from them; utterly and completely without trading one addiction for another. Help me see Your purpose and plan for my life. And if I must share in something, let it be in You. You are the Alpha and the Omega, the Beginning, and the End. Let me not have any other gods before You. In Jesus' name, Amen.

Stephen Scoggins

WRITE YOUR PRAYER

This week, pray for God to reveal to you where you are struggling with an addiction. There may be some subconscious behavior or object of addiction that you have not yet recognized as keeping you from becoming who God wants you to be. Listen for God's whisper in your ear and take heed. He will guide your Journey to worship and praise.

_____

_____

_____

_____

_____

_____

DRAW YOUR JOURNEY

You have been doing a lot of reflecting this week through your words and His Word. This page is your canvas to exercise the creative gifts He has given you. Use this page to illustrate this week's thought and prompt to gain the clarity needed to see your Journey from a different perspective.

Draw a picture of what you look like free from struggle. As God freed the Israelites, so He has freed you. Visualize how you look free from the addiction in your life. Through visualization comes actualization.

BUILDING PRINCIPLES

Congratulations!

You are well on your way to healing, understanding, and building a stronger relationship with God the Father.

Every step you take on your Journey, you are tearing down the walls that stand in your way. As you take these walls apart, use the blocks to build your foundation for success. This will be your guide as you intentionally shape the foundation for your success.

WEEK 4 BUILDING PRINCIPLE: ACCOUNTABILITY

We have been reflecting on our Journey and the addictions we cling to along the way. To release these addictions, we will build a foundation of accountability. As we approach week five, reflect on how you will hold yourself accountable. Through accountability, you will find that you can free yourself from any addiction hindering you from becoming the person Christ has designed for you to be.

_____

_____

_____

_____

_____

_____

_____

_____

"No test or temptation that comes your way is beyond the course of what others have had to face. All you need to remember is that God will never let you down; he'll never let you be pushed past your limit; he'll always be there to help you come through it."

1 Corinthians 10:13, The Message MSG

Week 4: Addiction vs. Sanctification

Week 5

Impatience May Come, but Grace Will Follow

Therefore I tell you, do not worry about your life, what you will eat or drink; or about your body, what you will wear. Is not life more important than food, and the body more than clothes?

Matthew 6:25, NIV

Week 5: Impatience May Come, but Grace Will Follow

Persevere in the Long Journey

Obstacle: Impatience and Immaturity
Building Principle: Perseverance

In this principle, we will explore the roles patience and maturity play in our ability to persevere and find contentment on our Journey. Remember last week when I said that rather than pray for a sudden miracle, we should pray for a gradual miracle? This may have sounded crazy in our world of instant gratification. Let me now take the time to elaborate on this thought.

In Journey Principle 5, I introduce impatience. It causes frustration, anger, resentment, and maybe even hostility. But what is it and where does it come from? I think that when most of us think about impatience, we think about a longing for the future. We feel excitement and anticipation for some upcoming experience that promises an emotional, physical, or material reward. However, we not only display impatience in reaching for the future, we also exhibit impatience to escape the present. Why do we want to escape the moment? Why do we want to rush to the future? More often than not, the answer is fear and greed. We either fear the moment or desire what we do not have. In both cases, impatience can create unnecessary stress, can negatively affect your relationships, and can keep you from finding and experiencing joy in life.

Scripture gives us many examples of how fear, anxiety, and impatience prevent us from moving forward. Take, for example, what Jesus tells us in Matthew 6: 25 NIV: "Therefore I tell you, do not worry about your life, what you will eat or drink; or about your body, what you will wear. Is not life more important than food, and the body more than clothes?"

Give an example of when you persevered along your Journey. When we take the time to write out our positive experience, it embeds itself into our mind and acts as a reserve for when we need it in our future. Write your story of perseverance and patience below.

_____

_____

_____

_____

NAOMI AND RUTH RETURN TO BETHLEHEM

Now that you have taken the time to review your story, we are going to dive into the Scripture. In the story of Naomi and Ruth, Ruth stays by the side of her mother-in-law. We all have family ties: some strong, some frayed, and some broken. In this situation, perseverance kept a strong bond from fraying. Read the story below and respond to the questions that follow as they apply to you.

Ruth 1: 6-17, NIV

"When Naomi heard in Moab that the Lord had come to the aid of his people by providing food for them, she and her daughters-in-law prepared to return home from there. With her two daughters-in-law, she left the place where she had been living and set out on the road that would take them back to the land of Judah.

Then Naomi said to her two daughters-in-law, 'Go back, each of you, to your mother's home. May the Lord show you kindness, as you have shown kindness to your dead husbands and to me. May the Lord grant that each of you will find rest in the home of another husband.'

Then she kissed them goodbye and they wept aloud and said to her, 'We will go back with you to your people.'

But Naomi said, 'Return home, my daughters. Why would you come with me? Am I going to have any more sons, who could become your husbands? Return home, my daughters; I am too old to have another husband. Even if I thought there was still hope for me – even if I had a husband tonight and then gave birth to sons – would you wait until they grew up? Would you remain unmarried for them? No, my daughters. It is more bitter for me than for you, because the Lord's hand has turned against me!'

At this, they wept aloud again. Then Orpah kissed her mother-in-law goodbye, but Ruth clung to her.

'Look,' said Naomi, 'your sister-in-law is going back to her people and her gods. Go back with her.'

But Ruth replied, 'Don't urge me to leave you or to turn back from you. Where you go I will go, and where you stay I will stay. Your people will be my people and your God my God. Where you die I will die, and there I will be buried. May the Lord deal with me, be it ever so severely, if even death separates you and me.'"

GOLDEN NUGGETS
Apply Ruth's Perseverance in Your Life

Reflect on Ruth's actions and see how you can apply these lessons in your life to grow in grace. In grace and patience, God will have the opportunity to reveal His map to you for your Journey.

People set goals for business, goals for retirement, goals for college; but they rarely set goals to strengthen their relationships, which is just as important as any other goal we place in our lives. This activity teaches us the importance of actively strengthening relationships.

Write what you feel you can take away and why you feel this is important to you. Our relationship with God begins when we are able to make the connection between Biblical stories and our lives, rather than waiting for our pastors or ministers to tell us. Use the questions below as an opportunity to practice finding the relevance on your own.

Where will you apply patience in your life this week?

_____

_____

Write the names of two people in your life whom you felt safe with and could trust, past or present.

_____

_____

Write 3 things you will do to strengthen current or future relationships:

_____

_____

_____

CHANGING THE MEANING

For the following words, write a definition that reflects how each word can make you stronger and help you on your Journey.

The Journey Principles talks about using adversity as a tool to build a better life. Here is your chance to practice and help change your relationships with these words. It will also help you to worship God with a learning heart. By changing these words from a negative to a positive point of view, you will change your relationship with them and build a new story around them. The importance is to build GRATITUDE for how they will sustain you.

Impatience

_____

_____

_____

Finished

_____

_____

_____

Perfect

_____

_____

_____

Journey Principle 5:
"Impatience May Come, but Grace Will Follow"

Read the story of Jacob in Genesis 32:1-33:20. Throughout this workbook, I will ask you to look at Jacob's story and find areas in your life where you may have experienced similar emotions or concerns. Take the time to sit back and reflect on those times.

JACOB WRESTLES

The same night he arose and took his two wives, his two female servants, and his eleven children, and crossed the ford of the Jabbok. He took them and sent them across the stream, and everything else that he had. And Jacob was left alone. And a man wrestled with him until the breaking of the day.

When the man saw that he did not prevail against Jacob, he touched his hip socket, and Jacob's hip was put out of joint as he wrestled with him. Then he said, "Let me go, for the day has broken." But Jacob said, "I will not let you go unless you bless me."

And he said to him, "What is your name?" And he said, "Jacob."

Then he said, "Your name shall no longer be called Jacob, but Israel, for you have striven with God and with men, and have prevailed."

Genesis 32: 22- 28, ESV

In this week's passage, Jacob sends all of his worldly possessions and loved ones across the river to focus on the Man he wrestles with. By clearing his space of distraction, Jacob made room to focus on God (even if it was a hand-to-hand struggle.) Bring to mind a time when you figuratively wrestled with God. What was He trying to tell you? How did the struggle impact your life?

We are blessed people of God. He provides for us in ways we don't even see. Is there an excess of something in your life that someone else could benefit from? Clear out an inch of your closet, storage room, or even electronics. Give freely to someone who is lacking. Pour your heart out to God and let Him know you are grateful.

SEARCHING THE SCRIPTURE FROM WITHIN

Now is the time to take God's Word into your hands and search for the passages that will guide you through your Journey and strengthen your prayer. In the paragraphs that follow, let His Word flow through you and speak to your Journey. By taking the time to review and record His holy Word, you will grow a greater awareness of His awesome power in your life.

1. So many times, we hold negative pictures of ourselves that are not only false, but have been put there by other people. These images can hold us hostage and can hinder our ability to love ourselves and others. Find a scripture that speaks of how God sees beauty in His people.

Scripture:

_____
_____

2. We have various relationships with our mothers and fathers. Some are beautiful and blessed and others are turbulent and tumultuous. In order to have a relationship based on God's truths, we need to read His Word. If you haven't had a good relationship with your mother or father, this is a great chance to start healing and create a new association with the words "mother" and "father." Discover scripture that brings positive meaning to these words for you.

Scripture:

_____
_____

3. What is your image of God? Seek scripture that helps you understand the difference between the Heavenly Father and our physical parents.

Scripture:

_____
_____

4. Our self-image is formed from many angles, from friends and family to personal experiences. How can you shape this into a more positive self-image? Find a passage or verse that heals the parts of your self-image that may be broken or torn and restores it to its original beauty.

Scripture:

_____
_____

QUESTIONS TO MOVE YOU FORWARD
WRITE YOUR ANSWERS ON THE LINES BELOW THE QUESTIONS

God gave us the gift of choice. Learning to ask yourself the right questions is something you have to practice. When we begin to develop this skill, that is when we can truly move forward in both our relationship with Him and in taking the next steps on our Journey.

Look at your most recent profile picture (social media of your choice). What are you trying to portray to your friends or followers?

_____

Seek comfort in understanding that your final portrait has not yet been painted. In your mind's eye, how would you like to see this picture come out?

_____

_____

We touched on how He will open up His family photo album with you when you come home to Him. What will you do this week to make a picture you will be proud to look at with Him?

_____

_____

Write a brief prayer to God asking for the patience to understand areas that you are still developing.

_____

_____

_____

SETTING YOUR PATH FOR GROWTH

"It is not that I have confidence, but I believe if I fail, so what? Now I have the chance to try again."

Maya Angelou

During these ten weeks and after, make sure that these goals are for YOU! Pray to God for guidance when you set your goals to match the path He has carved out for you.

We are at our halfway mark! How have the past four weeks been for you? Together, we have covered a lot of ground and made a lot of progress. Over the past four weeks, we have worked on goals to accomplish in the present.

I would like you to take a moment and flip back to week one. Recall that we set five goals and pick the next goal for the future (ideally, something you would like to accomplish over the next year).

Repeat this goal to yourself. Through this exercise, you are holding it in the forefront of your mind and you are more likely to meet your deadline.

Write it down here: _____

Have you ever seen a child learn to walk? There is a reason why we call them "toddlers." They stand, take a few wobbly steps on their new legs, and then they fall down. Yet, they get back up and keep trying!

I share this analogy with you because we need a reminder that as we are human, it is natural to stumble on the path to success. When we stumble and fall, it is imperative for us to get back up. Failure is a chance to learn!

Write down three ways you will persevere if you fall down:

_____

_____

_____

LIVING LIFE WITH GRACE

Here is an opportunity to realize that negative words and feelings have no power over you. At any moment and at any second, you can hand these words over to God. This activity is a practice to hand these feelings over to God and not wait for them to appear in the midst of a crisis. We will look at specific feelings and challenges that are both positive and negative. First, our focus will be on letting go of emotions that tie us down. Then we will close by practicing praise and gratitude to God by lifting up our accomplishments and challenges to the Lord.

Allow me to walk you through the first word:

Say the word "anxiety". Sit with the word, turn it over in your mind. Say: "I can hand this over to God. I will hand this over to God. I am handing over to God. I am." Now let out a breath of fresh air.

Repeat this process with the next word:

RELEASE FEELINGS THAT HOLD US DOWN

- Anxiety
- Guilt
- Hatred
- Jealousy
- Fear
- Violence

Now pause and take a breath. When you breathe out, let go of all those feelings and thank God for taking them from you.

Repeat this exercise with any feelings that you may be harboring that cause tightness in your chest. This can extend to a situation that causes you difficulty or a statement that is replaying in your mind. Let this negativity go.

PRAISE HIM WHEN WE'RE UP AND DOWN
UNDERSTAND THE ROLE ADVERSITY PLAYS IN OUR LIVES

In one way, we say that we are grateful to God that we can achieve things when they are not going as planned. On the other hand, we begin to understand that if we practice letting go and giving to God, we will live in joy and in peace. He will take care of the rest.

Week 5: Impatience May Come, but Grace Will Follow

To close this activity, we will visit our achievements and challenges. As you remember from week one, conflict generates growth! Thus, we give gratitude to the Lord for our obstacles because they make us who we are.

Start this exercise as follows: I am grateful for the people who love me in my life and I am grateful for the people who have taught me through sorrow. I can give gratitude to God. I am giving gratitude to God. I am grateful. I am.

Continue with the following phrases and add your own in the empty spaces!

I AM GRATEFUL FOR...

- Opportunity and challenges
- People who support me and people who test my boundaries
- My success and the mistakes I made along the way
- The opportunity to learn from my mistakes
- Season of joy and seasons of sorrow
- Times when I am flourishing
- _____
- _____
- _____

APPLYING THIS PRINCIPLE THROUGH PRAYER

Abba (Father,) thank You for this journey. Thank You for Your principles, Your wisdom and Your guidance. Thank You for showing me the road is long and the race is a marathon. Please calm my mind and heart and keep me steadfast in Your purpose. Please help my impatient nature, but never let me lose my passion for You or Your people. Help me know when I should just be still and know that You are God, and when You want me to act. In Jesus' name, Amen.

Stephen Scoggins

Week 5: Impatience May Come, but Grace Will Follow

WRITE YOUR PRAYER

In our impatience, we do a disservice to the Lord. Develop your prayer of serenity. How can you "let go and let God" in times of impatience? The Lord is all knowing and He alone knows the path we are destined to travel. Not only will you be praising the Lord by trusting in Him to take care of you, but you will be able to breathe and relax. Know that all things in Him are possible and all things in Him are good.

_____

_____

_____

_____

_____

_____

"If you read history you will find that the Christians who did the most for the present world were precisely those who thought the most of the next... It is since Christians have largely ceased to think of the other world that they have become so ineffective in this."

C.S. Lewis

Week 5: Impatience May Come, but Grace Will Follow

DRAW YOUR JOURNEY

You have been doing a lot of reflecting this week through your words and His Word. This page is your canvas to exercise the creative gifts He has given you. Use this page to illustrate this week's thought and prompt to gain the clarity needed to see your Journey from a different perspective.

Draw what your family photo album with God looks like. Pick a moment when you feel He has guided you and draw it here. Thank Him with your talents in that moment.

Week 5: Impatience May Come, but Grace Will Follow

BUILDING PRINCIPLES

Congratulations!

You are well on your way to healing, understanding, and building a stronger relationship with God the Father.

Every step you take on your Journey, you are tearing down the walls that stand in your way. As you take these walls apart, use the blocks to build your foundation for success. This will be your guide as you intentionally shape the foundation for your success.

WEEK 5 BUILDING PRINCIPLE: PERSEVERANCE

Find contentment in the Father and rest in His mercies! Now is the time to lay your foundation of perseverance. The past and present may threaten to shake you and tempt you to close your eyes until your future comes closer, with what you believe will comfort you or improve your situation. Keep your eyes open, stay the course, and work hard to see the blessings He has placed in your life and praise His name.

_____

_____

_____

_____

_____

_____

_____

_____

_____

"For the pagans run after all these things, and your heavenly Father knows that you need them. But seek first his kingdom and his righteousness, and all these things will be given to you as well."

Matthew 6:32-33, NIV

Week 5: Impatience May Come, but Grace Will Follow

Week 6

Sorrow is an Illusion

So we have come to know and to believe the love that God has for us. God is love, and whoever abides in love abides in God, and God abides in him.

1 John 4:16, ESV

The Greatest Love Story of All Time: His Compassion.

Obstacle: Sorrow
Building Principle: Compassion

Sorrow is not limited to death alone, but to loss as a whole. Consider a time when a relationship ended, when you were denied a job or when you found out a loved one must live with an incurable illness. Whether it happens gradually or all at once, sorrow can find itself knocking at your door. Unwittingly, we open the door and sorrow stays with us like a relative that just won't go home.

Soon, it becomes challenging to make decisions or even simple tasks.

Early on in childhood, I experienced the sorrow of losing a loved one. Shortly after my mother's attempted suicide, my Nanny became the official guardian of my brother and me. She put food in our bellies, clothes on our backs, a roof over our heads, and knowledge in our brains.

I am a blessed man to have known such love and compassion. After her battle with cancer, it was Nanny's time to see the Kingdom of God. I was very young at the time, but my heart ached and all that I could think about was how I wished I could have just one more hug!

Then I remembered her smile in the hospital and a wave of peace rushed over me and I knew that she was safe and no longer in pain. What a gift! My Nanny was now resting in Heaven.

Sorrow is an obstacle in our lives, just like the other five we have discussed. Just like ANY obstacle you come up against, sorrow is a chance for you to define yourself. When you confront it, you will gain a better understanding of who you want to be.

Sorrow is a chance for you to define yourself. If you confront it, it will allow you to better understand who you are. What will make sorrow a unique experience every time is that you will better understand areas in your life where you have room for improvement and what strengths you are blessed with. You will also gain an appreciation for time. Time will heal all wounds and give you the space needed to fine-tune patience and perseverance. Most importantly, sorrow is a reminder that life is short and you will recognize that every moment God gives us is precious.

JOSEPH MAKES HIMSELF KNOWN

Our first step on our sixth week will be to review the story of Joseph in Genesis. Before assuming his place as a man of immense power in Egypt, Joseph was merely one of twelve brothers and was sold into slavery by these same brothers. Years after this offense, Joseph's brothers came to Egypt to trade for grain as their family was suffering due to Canaan's severe famine. As the brothers came before Joseph, they did not recognize their kin. Through God's compassion, Joseph was able to make amends and show the compassion of Christ to his brothers. Read the following story and study the corresponding questions as they apply to your Journey.

Genesis 45:1-28, NIV

Then Joseph could no longer control himself before all his attendants, and he cried out, "Have everyone leave my presence!" So there was no one with Joseph when he made himself known to his brothers. And he wept so loudly that the Egyptians heard him, and Pharaoh's household heard about it.

Joseph said to his brothers, "I am Joseph! Is my father still living?" But his brothers were not able to answer him because they were terrified at his presence.

Then Joseph said to his brothers, "Come close to me." When they had done so, he said, "I am your brother Joseph, the one you sold into Egypt! And now, do not be distressed and do not be angry with yourselves for selling me here, because it was to save lives that God sent me ahead of you. For two years now there has been famine in the land, and for the next five years there will be no plowing and reaping. But God sent me ahead of you to preserve for you a remnant on earth and to save your lives by a great deliverance.

"So then, it was not you who sent me here, but God. He made me father to Pharaoh, lord of his entire household and ruler of all Egypt. Now hurry back to my father and say to him, 'This is what your son Joseph says: God has made me lord of all Egypt. Come down to me; don't delay. You shall live in the region of Goshen and be near me – you, your children and grandchildren, your flocks and herds, and all you have. I will provide for you there, because five years of famine are still to come. Otherwise you and your household and all who belong to you will become destitute.'

"You can see for yourselves, and so can my brother Benjamin, that it is really I who am speaking to you. Tell my father about all the honor accorded me in Egypt and about everything you have seen. And bring my father down here quickly."

Then he threw his arms around his brother Benjamin and wept, and Benjamin embraced him, weeping. And he kissed all his brothers and wept over them. Afterward his brothers talked with him.

When the news reached Pharaoh's palace that Joseph's brothers had come, Pharaoh and all his officials were pleased. Pharaoh said to Joseph, "Tell your brothers, 'Do this: Load your animals and return to the land of Canaan, and bring your father and your families back to me. I will give you the best of the land of Egypt and you can enjoy the fat of the land.'"

"You are also directed to tell them, 'Do this: Take some carts from Egypt for your children and your wives, and get your father and come. Never mind about your belongings, because the best of all Egypt will be yours.'"

So the sons of Israel did this. Joseph gave them carts, as Pharaoh had commanded, and he also gave them provisions for their

Week 6: Sorrow is an Illusion

journey. To each of them he gave new clothing, but to Benjamin he gave three hundred shekels of silver and five sets of clothes. And this is what he sent to his father: ten donkeys loaded with the best things of Egypt, and ten female donkeys loaded with grain and bread and other provisions for his journey. Then he sent his brothers away, and as they were leaving he said to them, "Don't quarrel on the way!"

So they went up out of Egypt and came to their father Jacob in the land of Canaan. They told him, "Joseph is still alive! In fact, he is ruler of all Egypt." Jacob was stunned; he did not believe them. But when they told him everything Joseph had said to them, and when he saw the carts Joseph had sent to carry him back, the spirit of their father Jacob revived. And Israel said, "I'm convinced! My son Joseph is still alive. I will go and see him before I die."

GOLDEN NUGGETS
LET JOSEPH'S TEARS FILL YOUR CUP OF COMPASSION

Think of the struggle Joseph's heart went through when he first saw the faces of not only his brothers, but also his betrayers. These men did not recognize the face of their own flesh and blood whom they had sold into slavery. Yet, Joseph broke into tears when he saw all of his brothers assembled. Joseph understood that it was God's will for him to grow into this powerful role and save God's people from famine.

We talk about having compassion for others and loving our neighbors as we love ourselves, and yet we experience fights and transgressions that seem impossible to mend. When you go through these times, pray for compassion to wash through your heart and let His words pour out as the healing balm needed to make things right.

Our relationship with God begins when we are able to make the connection between Biblical stories and our lives, rather than waiting for our pastors or ministers to tell us. Use this moment to practice finding the meaning God has hidden between the words for you.

How have past transgressions built you into a more compassionate person?

_____

_____

How will you practice compassion this week?

_____

_____

Week 6: Sorrow is an Illusion

Write 3 things you will do to mend current or future relationships damaged by wrongs done unto you:

_____

_____

_____

CHANGING THE MEANING

For the following words, write a definition that reflects how each word can make you stronger and help you on your Journey.

The Journey Principles talks about using adversity as a tool to build a better life. Here is your chance to practice and help change your relationships with these words. It will also help you to worship God with a learning heart. By changing these words from a negative to a positive point of view, you will change your relationship with them and build a new story around them. The importance is to build GRATITUDE for how they will sustain you.

Sorrow

_____

_____

_____

Grief

_____

_____

_____

Abandonment

_____

_____

_____

Journey Principle 6:
"Sorrow is an Illusion"

Read the story of Jacob in Genesis 32:1-33:20. Throughout this workbook, I will ask you to look at Jacob's story and find areas in your life where you may have experienced similar emotions or concerns. Take the time to sit back and reflect on those times.

Week 6: Sorrow is an Illusion

JACOB IS BLESSED

Then Jacob asked Him, "Please tell me your name." But He said, "Why is it that you ask my name?" And there He blessed him. So Jacob called the name of the place Peniel, saying, "For I have seen God face to face, and yet my life has been delivered."

The sun rose upon him as he passed Penuel, limping because of his hip. Therefore to this day the people of Israel do not eat the sinew of the thigh that is on the hip socket, because He touched the socket of Jacob's hip on the sinew of the thigh.

And Jacob lifted up his eyes and looked, and behold, Esau was coming, and four hundred men with him. So he divided the children among Leah and Rachel and the two female servants. And he put the servants with their children in front, then Leah with her children, and Rachel and Joseph last of all.

Genesis 32: 29-33, 33: 1-2, ESV

After wrestling with God and giving himself unto Him, Jacob rejoins his group and continues his journey. Similarly, we continue our Journey. Think about a time you have been separated from your loved ones and came back to them, only different. Coming back to your community after a change can be difficult. Reflect on this time and how you learned to communicate this difference to your community of loved ones. How did they accept you?

Community is very important. With the support of others, we can make it through the roughest of storms. Are you experiencing sorrow or do you know someone who is? Go help a neighbor this week. Rake their yard, shovel their driveway, roll their trash bins up to their home, or even bring over a casserole! Let your neighbor know that you care. Pour your heart out to God and let Him know you are grateful.

SEARCHING THE SCRIPTURE FROM WITHIN

Now is the time to take God's Word into your hands and search for the passages that will guide you through your Journey and strengthen your prayer. In the paragraphs that follow, let His Word flow through you and speak to your Journey. By taking the time to review and record His holy Word, you will grow a greater awareness of His awesome power in your life.

Look at the story of Joseph and find the scripture where God tells you the purpose behind the sorrow. This is all to lead us to our victories. If we search scripture and learn from stories and others, we will learn that God is always there for us and teaches us to help others.

1. Was there a wound inflicted upon you by someone that you are still healing from? In our story of Joseph, we saw how a man who was sold into slavery by his own brothers was able to forgive and understand how these trespasses led him to do God's work. Now look at the Word to find a scripture that places the balm on your wound to help you grow from your experience into the person God plans for you to be.

Scripture:

_____

_____

2. When you feel abandoned, remember that He is with you always and will never leave your side. Search for scripture that shows God's promise to be stand alongside His people.

Scripture:

_____

_____

3. How have you been deceived by others along your Journey? When we believe we are being told the truth and led with good intention, only to find out otherwise, our trust in others is shattered. Look for scripture that speaks of staying on the true path.

Scripture:

_____

_____

4. When you are feeling tremendous sorrow, it may seem like there is no way out. Take heart and know that God raises those who feel anchored to their sorrow and wipes their tears. Seek out scripture that shows His compassion for the sorrow of His people. Know that He has compassion for you.

Scripture:

_____

_____

QUESTIONS TO MOVE YOU FORWARD
WRITE YOUR ANSWERS ON THE LINES BELOW THE QUESTIONS.

God gave us the gift of choice. Learning to ask yourself the right questions is something you have to practice. When we begin to develop this skill, that is when we can truly move forward in both our relationship with Him and in taking the next steps on our Journey.

Who are three people you feel have wronged you and what is one action you will take to extend compassion for each?

1. _____

2. _____

3. _____

How will you petition God for the blessing of understanding and compassion?

_____

_____

Name one step you will take this week to mend one broken relationship.

_____

_____

Reflect on a time when you have suffered a season of sorrow. What lessons did you learn from this season and how have those lessons shaped your heart in compassion?

_____

_____

_____

SETTING YOUR PATH FOR GROWTH

"Heart and mind overcome all."

Dan Henderson

During these ten weeks and after, make sure that these goals are for YOU! Pray to God for guidance when you set your goals to match the path He has carved out for you.

This week, our goal setting session will look a little different. Below is a "Life Wheel." As you can see, each section of the wheel identifies different areas of our lives for which we set goals. Take some time to identify which areas of your life you would like to improve on and set goals here. Note that you are not expected to fill slots 1-10 for every section! It is natural for some sections to be heavier than others.

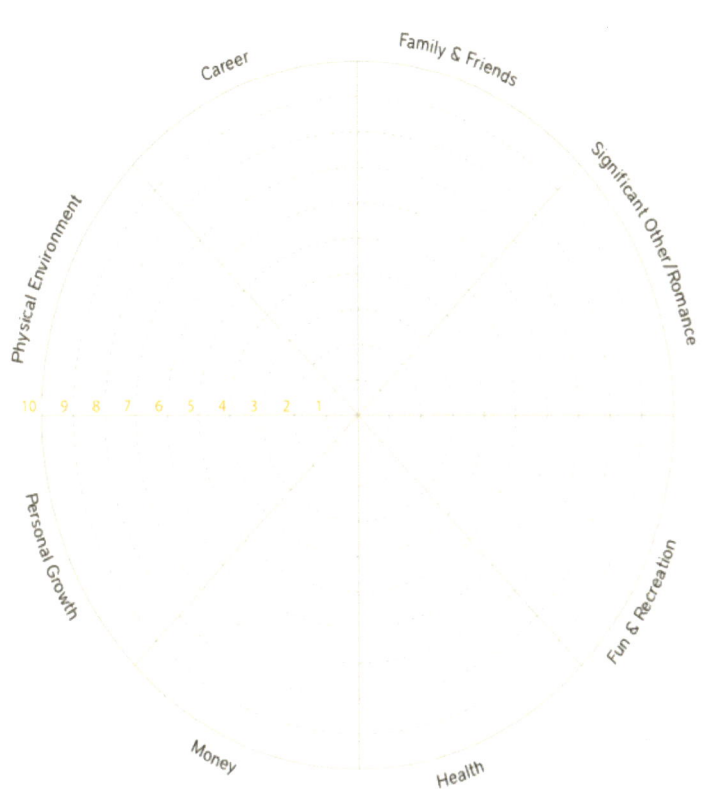

Once you have your Life Wheel completed, identify two areas of life where you can set a goal that will support your compassion.

If sorrow is an illusion and compassion is our building block, then we must set goals to let go of sorrow and embrace compassion.

Identify one goal to open your heart to compassion:

_____
_____
_____

What are two steps you can take this week to achieve goals in your Life Wheel and what can you do to move towards compassion in these goals? Then apply compassion to yourself and others as you achieve your goals.

1. _____
2. _____

Week 6: Sorrow is an Illusion

APPLYING THIS PRINCIPLE THROUGH PRAYER

Father, how great is Your plan. How great is Your mission for my life. I know that You bring forth all things for Your plan and You waste nothing. Please walk with me now releasing in my heart and mind all sorrow and pain. Please reveal to me how You want it to be a part of my walk, plan, and testimony. Remove doubt from me and cast it away in the deepest sea, never to be seen again. I can now see sorrow has no purpose in my life any longer, and I can see how the evil one has made it a plan to keep me from that which You created me for. Help me to realize not my worth in others, but my worth in You! In Jesus' name, Amen.

Stephen Scoggins

WRITE YOUR PRAYER

Sorrow comes in many forms throughout our lives. Whether one of our loved ones has departed to Heaven or we have lost a job or are feeling as if everything is going wrong; God will never bestow a weight on us that we cannot carry. How are you praying for compassion this week? For we are so loved by our Creator that He sent His only Son down to walk among us. During your prayer, practice praise for the compassion others have shown you and aspire to extend the same to others.

_____

_____

_____

_____

_____

_____

Week 6: Sorrow is an Illusion

DRAW YOUR JOURNEY

You have been doing a lot of reflecting this week through your words and His Word. This page is your canvas to exercise the creative gifts He has given you. Use this page to illustrate this week's thought and prompt to gain the clarity needed to see your Journey from a different perspective.

Pick up your pen or pencil and prepare your heart for compassion. Draw a picture of how your day-to-day will look when the cloud of sorrow clears. Will your shoulders feel lighter? Will a smile grace your lips? By making this drawing, you will be able to envision a life where the compassion of Christ blesses you.

Week 6: Sorrow is an Illusion

BUILDING PRINCIPLES

Congratulations!

You are well on your way to healing, understanding, and building a stronger relationship with God the Father.

Every step you take on your Journey, you are tearing down the walls that stand in your way. As you take these walls apart, use the blocks to build your foundation for success. This will be your guide as you intentionally shape the foundation for your success.

WEEK 6 BUILDING PRINCIPLE: COMPASSION

This week may have been one of the most difficult we've traveled through so far. Take a moment as we bring Week 6 to a close and reflect on the lessons we learned about how compassion combats sorrow. Record these lessons so that when you feel sorrow and depression come upon you, you will remember that His compassion will protect you from these negative emotions.

_____

_____

_____

_____

_____

_____

_____

_____

_____

_____

Gracious is the LORD, and righteous; Yes, our God is compassionate.

Psalms 116:5, NASB

Week 6: Sorrow is an Illusion

Week 7

Pride's Prison

And they said to one another, "Come, let us cast lots that we may know on whose account this evil has come upon us." So they cast lots, and the lot fell on Jonah. Then they said to him, "Tell us on whose account this evil has come upon us. What is your occupation? And where do you come from? What is your country? And of what people are you?" And he said to them, "I am a Hebrew, and I fear the Lord, the God of heaven, who made the sea and the dry land." Then the men were exceedingly afraid and said to him, "What is this that you have done!" For the men knew that he was fleeing from the presence of the Lord, because he had told them.

Jonah 1: 7-10, ESV

Find Wisdom Within Humility

Obstacle: Pride
Building Principle: Humility

We live in a society that is in a race. A race to have more, do more, or be better than those around us. It's unfortunate, but many people can only perceive their value in comparison to others. They are so lost. They don't know who they are or what they stand for. They are so discontent with what they have that the only way they can experience joy or happiness is by creating a mindset that lifts their circumstance above others.

This mindset is not joy! No matter how much you try to fool yourself, this is not happiness. It is pride and an extremely unhealthy way to assign value to one's life.

While our society thrives on social media and parties to boast our prideful nature, this is not the first time (nor the last time) that pride has plagued God's children.

Now, it is important to distinguish the differences between good pride and bad pride. Pride can be a driving force that pushes you toward future success and can inspire your dreams and creativity. Yet, there is a thin line. When this line is crossed, we are no longer content with our achievements. When praise moves from simply being accepted to being sought out, we begin to look outside of our own Journey and begin to compare ourselves with those around us.

Think of a verse or a parable from the Bible where pride was the downfall of those men and women.

Write down the verse here:

_____

_____

What I would like you to do next is recall why this particular verse spoke to you. What is it about these words that demonstrate the negative effects of pride and how can you use this lesson from the Bible to keep you from falling prey to the same ordeal?

_____

_____

Take a moment to review Luke 18: 9-14 with me:

The Pharisee and the Tax Collector:

He also told this parable to some people who trusted in themselves that they were righteous, and treated others with contempt: "Two men went up into the temple to pray, one a Pharisee and the other a tax collector. The Pharisee stood and was praying this to himself: 'God, I thank You that I am not like other people: swindlers, unjust, adulterers, or even like this tax collector. I fast twice a week; I pay tithes of all that I get.' But the tax collector, standing some distance away, was even unwilling to lift up his eyes to heaven, but was beating his breast, saying, 'God, be merciful to me, the sinner!' I tell you, this man went to his house justified rather than the other; for everyone who exalts himself will be humbled, but he who humbles himself will be exalted.

When I read this passage, I can't help but think of the Pharisee as the Facebook friend who "checks-in" while volunteering. This friend does not exalt in the "good deed" or simply let their actions be pure and good of heart. They turn something whole and beautiful into something that is self-serving.

What similarities do you see between the Pharisee and yourself?

_____

_____

How can you strive to humble yourself like the tax collector?

_____

_____

In what settings do you find yourself comparing yourselves to others?

_____

_____

In these settings, how can you find joy in your life without bringing others down?

_____

_____

If we all lived in the humble image of Christ, what would the world look like? Think, if you will, about living a life where you do not feel the need to impress those around you, a life where you are content with yourself.

Let's take a moment to consider this in two parts: your physical surroundings and your relationship with others.

1. Physical:
   - If you did not have to worry about the judgment or contempt of others, would you have less stuff or fewer material possessions?
   - Would you drive a different car or live in a different house?
   - How do you think that living a more modest lifestyle would impact you financially and how would that influence your life?

Week 7: Pride's Prison

2. Relational:
   - How would changing your approach to one of humility and respect change the relationships in your life?
   - Would you judge people less and appreciate people more?
   - How might it affect your ability to forgive?
   - Would you become an active listener?

Identify two ways in both your physical surroundings and your relationships that you are going to implement humility this week. By making this pledge, you will be taking the first steps to living an empowered life.

1. Physical

_____

_____

2. Relational

_____

_____

Now that we have come to an understanding, let's go put our submission into action by serving, not for personal gain, but rather with a true heart to help our brothers and sisters in Christ.

ACTION STEPS TO FIND HUMILITY

1. **Value others** and their perspectives. We must understand that each person brings their own special gifts to the table. Every person has something valuable to contribute and so every person deserves respect. We have talked about iron sharpening iron and the war of conflicting ideas. The best way for us to grow as individuals and as a collective is to learn from each other's strengths and to build off of them.

2. **Recognize your weaknesses**. John C. Maxwell states, "Pride deafens us to the advice or warnings of those around us." When you humbly accept your limitations, it opens up your heart and mind to receive wisdom from those around you.

3. **Don't brag about yourself**. Remember to focus on improving yourself in your Journey and not living a life in comparison with others.

CHANGING THE MEANING

For the following words, write a definition that reflects how each word can make you stronger and help you on your Journey.

The Journey Principles talks about using adversity as a tool to build a better life. Here is your chance to practice and help change your relationships with these words. It will also help you to worship God with a learning heart. By changing these words from a negative to a positive point of view, you will change your relationship with them and build a new story around them. The importance is to build GRATITUDE for how they will sustain you.

False

_____

_____

_____

Prideful

_____

_____

_____

Comparison

_____

_____

_____

Journey Principle 7:
"Pride's Prison"

Read the story of Jacob in Genesis 32:1-33:20. Throughout this workbook, I will ask you to look at Jacob's story and find areas in your life where you may have experienced similar emotions or concerns. Take the time to sit back and reflect on those times.

ESAU

He himself went on before them, bowing himself to the ground seven times, until he came near to his brother.

But Esau ran to meet him and embraced him and fell on his neck and kissed him, and they wept. And when Esau lifted up his eyes and saw the women and children, he said, "Who are these with you?" Jacob said, "The children whom God has graciously given your servant." Then the servants drew near, they and their children, and bowed down.

Leah likewise and her children drew near and bowed down. And last Joseph and Rachel drew near, and they bowed down. Esau said, "What do you mean by all this company that I met?" Jacob answered, "To find favor in the sight of my lord." But Esau said, "I have enough, my brother; keep what you have for yourself." Jacob said, "No, please, if I have found favor in your sight, then accept my present from my hand. For I have seen your face, which is like seeing the face of God, and you have accepted me."

Genesis 33: 3-10, ESV

Has there been a time when you were tempted to be prideful, but you bit your tongue, bowed your head, and fell to your knees? Recall this experience and remember how your heart felt during that moment and the following morning. By choosing to be humble, what were the reactions of those around you?

Practice humility this week and pay it forward. Take the kindness that has been shown to you throughout your life and return it to the world. When you are buying a coffee or groceries, pay for the person behind you. The unexpected kindness you show them will fill your heart with joy and carry you through your Journey (just as it will for them!). Pour your heart out to God and let Him know you are grateful.

SEARCHING THE SCRIPTURE FROM WITHIN

Now is the time to take God's Word into your hands and search for the passages that will guide you through your Journey and strengthen your prayer. In the paragraphs that follow, let His Word flow through you and speak to your Journey. By taking the time to review and record His holy Word, you will grow a greater awareness of His awesome power in your life.

1. Look to Proverbs to see how pride can be destructive, but see how humility leads us to God's wisdom. Find a verse that you can hold with you as you travel your Journey and look to it in times when society looks down on the humble.

Scripture:

_____

_____

2. Remember that we are all created in the image of God. Knowing this truth, our brothers and sisters in Christ are to be loved and valued as we love and value Him. Search for scripture which speaks to how we can love and value our brothers and sisters, even when their actions challenge us to do so.

Scripture:

_____

_____

3. To avoid the clutches of pride, be inspired by humbling yourself. Look to Scripture for this inspiration. Look at these Biblical examples for guidance when you feel tempted by pride.

Scripture:

_____

_____

4. In a world where our self-worth is held up against our possessions, position, and money, we must remember that it is He who has blessed us with everything we have; nothing of this world goes with us when we enter the Kingdom of God. Uncover a passage that demonstrates the importance of remembering God's promise of eternal life. Reflect on how this can help you remain steadfast when others boast.

Scripture:

_____

_____

QUESTIONS TO MOVE YOU FORWARD
WRITE YOUR ANSWERS ON THE LINES BELOW THE QUESTIONS.

God gave us the gift of choice. Learning to ask yourself the right questions is something you have to practice. When we begin to develop this skill, that is when we can truly move forward in both our relationship with Him and in taking the next steps on our Journey.

Are you living your life in comparison with others? Why do you think you are doing this?

_____

_____

Identify 3 ways to engage in competition with yourself to become a more "superior" you instead of comparing yourself to others.

1. _____

2. _____

3. _____

How do you think humility might affect your ability to confront obstacles?

_____

_____

How can you demonstrate humility consistently?

_____

_____

Reflect on how our society would change if fewer people felt misunderstood, free from judgment, and more confident in expressing emotion. What would this look like?

Week 7: Pride's Prison

SETTING YOUR PATH FOR GROWTH

"Efforts and courage are not enough without purpose and direction."

John F. Kennedy

During these ten weeks and after, make sure that these goals are for YOU! Pray to God for guidance when you set your goals to match the path He has carved out for you.

I am going to tell you something that will transform the way you follow your path to success: God has a plan for us that may not always align with our plan, and our goals change over time – that's okay!

We have been discussing pride and how it can keep us from strengthening our relationship with God the Father. On occasion, we get so laser-focused on our path to success that we forget Who set us on this path in the first place. When you feel that you keep failing at a goal after approaching it time and time again, it may be time to step back.

Take a close look at your goals. Have you prayed over your goals for guidance? Has He led you to this path? Name three ways in which your current goal leads you to strengthen your relationship with Him:

_____

_____

_____

Now that you have examined this goal, write one encouraging statement to yourself to keep working toward the objective:

_____

_____

_____

APPLYING THIS PRINCIPLE THROUGH PRAYER

Father, You have always said pride comes before a fall. Remove pride from my life. Grant in me a clean heart and right spirit, never denying my heart from any of Your love, grace, and mercy You have to offer. Help me to serve, and not be selfish. Help me to grow in washing the feet of others as You wash my heart of pride. Clean me, oh Lord. Restore me, oh Lord. Let pride not tear me from You, from others or my utter and complete healing. In Jesus' name, Amen.

Stephen Scoggins

WRITE YOUR PRAYER

Throughout the week, we have focused on how pride can lead to our corruption and can block us from making progress in our Journey. Take the time to write your prayer to God and ask Him to open your heart to humility. How can accepting a humble view lead you on your Journey? I hope that this will lead you to a heightened awareness of the blessings God has placed in your life and lead you to richer praise.

_____

_____

_____

_____

_____

_____

DRAW YOUR JOURNEY

You have been doing a lot of reflecting this week through your words and His Word. This page is your canvas to exercise the creative gifts He has given you. Use this page to illustrate this week's thought and prompt to gain the clarity needed to see your Journey from a different perspective.

Remember how we talked about your physical and relational humility? Draw what a more humble environment looks like to you. Is your garage a little less stuffed? Have you donated unused possessions to charity? Or are your words simply in praise of others as opposed to self-promoting? By drawing this, you will show Him that you are ready to accept His purpose and gift into your life.

Week 7: Pride's Prison

BUILDING PRINCIPLES

Congratulations!

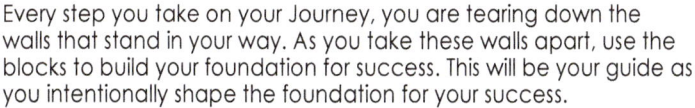

You are well on your way to healing, understanding, and building a stronger relationship with God the Father.

Every step you take on your Journey, you are tearing down the walls that stand in your way. As you take these walls apart, use the blocks to build your foundation for success. This will be your guide as you intentionally shape the foundation for your success.

WEEK 7 BUILDING PRINCIPLE: HUMILITY

Reflect on how humility will deepen your relationship with God. Remember, through Him, all things are possible! We can take comfort in knowing that we do not need to hold up our lives against our peers to know that we are making progress. The only comparison we need to make is looking back on the steps we have taken in our Journey. How far have you come? What accomplishments are you proud of (and rightly so!)? Most importantly, how can you praise His name for having a hand in your Journey? Write your thoughts down here and congratulate yourself on YOUR progress.

_____

_____

_____

_____

_____

_____

_____

For everyone who exalts himself will be humbled, and he who humbles himself will be exalted.

Luke 14:11, ESV

Week 8

Guilt Has Had Us Long Enough

Therefore, there is now no condemnation for those who are in Christ Jesus, because through Christ Jesus the law of the Spirit who gives life has set you free from the law of sin and death.

Romans 8:1-2, NIV

God's Efforts are Strongest When Our Efforts are Useless

Obstacle: Guilt
Building Principle: Grace

A season of my life where I suffered the vice of guilt stemmed from the fall of 1996. I took on work for a man named Steve Myrick. Steve was largely a father figure for me. During the time when I did siding for Steve, I struggled deeply with depression. I was working on a job one day and I started crying, to the point where I got up and went on a walk... all the way back to the single-wide trailer that I was living in at the time.

From that day, it took nearly a year for me to face Steve again. My father went to Steve on my behalf and was able to get Steve to let me back on the framing crew. I worked hard for Steve and picked up the slack where I saw it. I did a house a week, working fourteen-hour days, seven days a week. But it was my guilt and my desire to make amends for what I had done to Steve that allowed me to step up and take on that job by myself.

Guilt...

This word hangs heavily over our heads, but it can also lead us to greatness. For me, I grappled with the guilt from walking out on Steve for over a year, but it ended up leading me to one of the biggest blessings of my life! I encourage you to learn from my Journey and not wait a year to make amends. Has something happened between you and a loved one long ago? It's never too late to make things right.

If we were keeping score, I technically never asked Steve for forgiveness and technically, he never told me that I was forgiven. But I showed my remorse in my actions and he showed me forgiveness in grace. Sometimes, actions speak louder than words. Is this the same for you? Would something as simple as mowing your neighbor's yard show your contrition?

Write down one thing you can say or do today to mend any bridges that may be burned in your life. By writing this down here, you are promising to take the steps needed to make the situation right. For when we enter the Kingdom of God, we will want to greet (and be greeted by) others with joy! It all starts here.

Please remember as we go forward in week eight that you have been sanctified in Christ! Remember that there is no condemnation for those who remain in Him.

Guilt is similar to regret, conviction, and shame, but they are not exactly the same. Look at the differences laid out below to see how guilt distinguishes itself from its cousins: regret, conviction, and shame.

Guilt	Regret
Remorse for intentional wrongs "I meant to do it." Aware of wrongdoing at the time	Remorse for accidental wrongs "If I knew, I'd have done differently" Unaware of wrongdoing at the time
Guilt	**Conviction**
Comes from inside May be unaware Secretly knows guilt	Comes from outside Feel conviction from God or conscience Declared guilty by a court
Guilt	**Shame**
"I Did..." Sees bad behavior to change Can be resolved or paid for	"I Am..." Sees bad person to condemn Always feels damaged or disqualified

So how can we make the choice to grow from guilt in a healthy way? We first need to distinguish a healthy response from an unhealthy response. Review the table below to gain the understanding that will help you use your guilt as a compass on your Journey.

Healthy Response	Unhealthy Response
Accept Responsibility	Blame Others
Listen Humbly	Deny Reality
Seek Restitution	Strike Again
Release Guilt	Torture Self

Holding onto feelings of guilt is similar to holding a grudge: both are forms of a stubborn and unforgiving heart. A grudge is external, but your guilt is INTERNAL. We must reset the score in our relationships to get ourselves off of our own "bad list" and rejoice in the blank slate.

Take the time to reflect inwardly on the following questions. Identify the baggage you may be carrying with you and what you need to do to lighten your load.

Week 8: Guilt Has Had Us Long Enough

What guilt am I holding onto?

_____
_____
_____

How can I accept responsibility, listen, restore relationships, and release guilt?

_____
_____
_____

How am I currently processing guilt?

_____
_____
_____

How can I receive grace and seek growth through my guilt?

_____
_____
_____

ISAIAH'S COMMISSION

Isaiah felt the pain and despair of guilt, he cried out to God for help. Isaiah saw God as very holy and he witnessed God's great mercy. Our healing starts with God's holiness and mercy. If we put a separation between God's Holiness and His mercy we will get the wrong idea about God. Throughout life we may find ourselves like Isaiah crying out to God "Woe to me! I am ruined! For I am a man of unclean lips, and I live among a people of unclean lips, and my eyes have seen the King, the Lord Almighty". May Isaiah's experience be a lifeline to your knowing God's holiness and mercy. Amen!

Isaiah 6:1-7, NIV

In the year that King Uzziah died, I saw the Lord, high and exalted, seated on a throne; and the train of his robe filled the temple. Above him were seraphim, each with six wings: With two wings they covered their faces, with two they covered their feet, and with two they were flying. And they were calling to one another:

"Holy, holy, holy is the Lord Almighty; the whole earth is full of his glory."At the sound of their voices the doorposts and thresholds shook and the temple was filled with smoke.

Week 8: Guilt Has Had Us Long Enough

"Woe to me!" I cried. "I am ruined! For I am a man of unclean lips, and I live among a people of unclean lips, and my eyes have seen the King, the Lord Almighty."

Then one of the seraphim flew to me with a live coal in his hand, which he had taken with tongs from the altar. With it he touched my mouth and said, "See, this has touched your lips; your guilt is taken away and your sin atoned for."

God desires to give us freedom. He wants us to have the joy of His grace. When we feel guilty and unworthy, we know that God is holy and merciful. God will help us.

GOLDEN NUGGETS
Using the Meaning of Isaiah to Build Inspirational Go-To Support

Reflect on Isaiah 6:1-7 and see how you can apply the lessons to your life and grow in grace. Have you ever felt your sins were too heavy to bear? Have you ever turned away from God, believing you were unworthy of His love and mercy? In grace and mercy, God will reveal His love for you during your Journey.

This activity teaches us the importance of having tools and resources that encourage us to turn to our Lord and Savior Jesus Christ, and access the mercy and love He freely gives us.

Our relationship with God is strengthened when we know how to build support around us. Rather than waiting for something good to happen in your life, this activity reminds you to turn to God and know you have already won. We will use music and literature to make the connection between Biblical stories and your life.

Pick five of your favorite Christian songs and authors, so when you are feeling down, you have a resource to go to. Allow your literature and music to help you access God's love.

List 5 Christian Songs that lift your spirit:

1. _____
2. _____
3. _____
4. _____
5. _____

Week 8: Guilt Has Had Us Long Enough

List 5 Christian authors who inspire you:

1. _____
2. _____
3. _____
4. _____
5. _____

List 5 ways God has shown He loves you today:

1. _____
2. _____
3. _____
4. _____
5. _____

CHANGING THE MEANING

For the following words, write a definition that reflects how each word can make you stronger and help you on your Journey.

The Journey Principles talks about using adversity as a tool to build a better life. Here is your chance to practice and help change your relationships with these words. It will also help you to worship God with a learning heart. By changing these words from a negative to a positive point of view, you will change your relationship with them and build a new story around them. The importance is to build GRATITUDE for how they will sustain you.

Guilt

_____
_____
_____

Regret

_____
_____
_____

Week 8: Guilt Has Had Us Long Enough

Shame

_____
_____
_____

Journey Principle 8:
"Guilt Has Had Us Long Enough"

Read the story of Jacob in Genesis 32:1-33:20. Throughout this workbook, I will ask you to look at Jacob's story and find areas in your life where you may have experienced similar emotions or concerns. Take the time to sit back and reflect on those times.

JACOB TRAVELS TO SEIR

... For I have seen your face, which is like seeing the face of God, and you have accepted me.

Please accept my blessing that is brought to you, because God has dealt graciously with me, and because I have enough." Thus he urged him, and he took it.

Then Esau said, "Let us journey on our way, and I will go ahead of you." But Jacob said to him, "My lord knows that the children are frail, and that the nursing flocks and herds are a care to me. If they are driven hard for one day, all the flocks will die."

"Let my lord pass on ahead of his servant, and I will lead on slowly, at the pace of the livestock that are ahead of me and at the pace of the children, until I come to my lord in Seir."

Genesis 33: 10-14, ESV

Esau, who had plenty, was reluctant to accept Jacob's gifts and did not want Jacob to submit himself as a servant. Yet Jacob persisted and expressed that it was God's will for him to extend the grace of God. When have you been able to show grace? How did you accept this into your heart?

Jacob's heart implored him to extend this gift to Esau. What action has your heart been wanting you to take? This week, take the action! Go on a hike, visit family, write the first chapter of your novel, or make someone dinner. Whatever you have been wanting to do, but keep finding reason not to, do it this week! Pour your heart out to God and let Him know you are grateful.

SEARCHING THE SCRIPTURE FROM WITHIN

Now is the time to take God's Word into your hands and search for the passages that will guide you through your Journey and strengthen your prayer. In the paragraphs that follow, let His Word flow through you and speak to your Journey. By taking the time to

review and record His holy Word, you will grow a greater awareness of His awesome power in your life.

1. Feeling guilt is part of being human. We are imperfect and we make mistakes. From Journey Principle 8, we know that guilt is the product of consciously acting in the wrong. However, knowing that we have made a mistake is the first step toward making things right. Find scripture that speaks of repentance and how this cleanses us of our sins.

Scripture:

_____

_____

2. More than knowing we have acted in the wrong, we must accept our responsibility for the transgression to truly make amends. Think on this and find a passage that will give you the courage to take ownership of past and present actions that have caused you guilt.

Scripture:

_____

_____

3. Confessing our sins to those whom we have done wrong unto is the next step, but then we must seek restitution. When have you repaid in full (with or without interest) someone you have wronged? What was the result of this? Look for scripture that shows how restitution can mend any broken bridges and heal old wounds.

Scripture:

_____

_____

4. After we have confessed and sought restitution, it is time to release the guilt. God does not require that we carry this burden with us after making amends. He wants us to go on our Journey and learn from these mistakes. Discover scripture that helps you release any guilt you may be harboring and seek out God's grace.

Scripture:

_____

_____

Week 8: Guilt Has Had Us Long Enough

QUESTIONS TO MOVE YOU FORWARD
WRITE YOUR ANSWERS ON THE LINES BELOW THE QUESTIONS.

God gave us the gift of choice. Learning to ask yourself the right questions is something you have to practice. When we begin to develop this skill, that is when we can truly move forward in both our relationship with Him and in taking the next steps on our Journey.

Name three times in which you have felt heavy with guilt, be it past or present.

1. _____

2. _____

3. _____

How have you sought restitution?

_____

_____

How did letting go of these burdens allow you to move forward in your relationships with your loved ones and with Him?

_____

_____

What are two ways in which you will praise God this week for His grace?

1. _____

2. _____

SETTING YOUR PATH FOR GROWTH

"No one knows how far his strengths go, until he has tried them."

Johann Wolfgang von Goethe

During these ten weeks and after, make sure that these goals are for YOU! Pray to God for guidance when you set your goals to match the path He has carved out for you.

Successful people know what their natural born strengths are and how to tailor them toward accomplishing their goals. We are going to examine how your God-given gifts can be the keys to your success.

Week 8: Guilt Has Had Us Long Enough

Write down five strengths or talents you have:

1. _____
2. _____
3. _____
4. _____
5. _____

How can you use these strengths to your advantage?

_____
_____
_____

After reflecting on how you can use these strengths, apply these steps and test them out! If it doesn't work the first time, awesome! Now you know that you need to find another approach.

Make it a goal to exercise this activity over the next few weeks and praise His name for the gifts He has given you.

ACTION STEPS FOR LEARNING TO OPERATE IN GRACE

1. **Forgive** – This is the most important aspect of grace. Forgive in love! We know that forgiveness is just as much about personal healing as it is about the repairing of a relationship. Remember your own feelings of guilt when dealing with others and be quick to forgive.
2. **Serve** – Learn to look for the ways in which you can help others. We all have needs. Don't be afraid to look for the ways that you can really impact someone else's life.
3. **Speak life** – Yes, I stole this from one Mr. Toby Mac, but there is a profound truth in knowing how your words can affect others. Show grace in your communication and "speak hope, speak love, and speak life!"
4. **Show gratitude** – Operating in grace means being gracious. A no-brainer, right? Go out of your way to show thanks and appreciation to others. Respond to grace with grace.
5. **Turn the other cheek** – This is most definitely the hardest one, but grace can sometimes have the biggest impact when it is undeserved. Maintaining a graceful spirit is one of the best ways to overcome conflict!
6. **Extend Grace** – I've heard someone define grace from God as being given what we haven't earned. Isn't that the coolest thing about our God, His giving us His unconditional love despite our being undeserving? We don't have to earn salvation; it's free of charge. Amazing grace indeed! When that type of mercy and grace has been extended to you, how can you not glorify Him by extending it to others? Just as compassion is a huge tool for sharing Christ with others, extending grace is a tremendous way to let Him shine through you. However, though many Christians have accepted Christ, they are still overcome with guilt.

Please remember that you have been sanctified in Christ. Remember that there is no condemnation for those who remain in Him. In Max Lucado's book, *Grace for the Moment*, he reminds us that "when He says we're forgiven, let's unload the guilt. When He says we're valuable, let's believe Him. When He says we're provided for, let's stop worrying. God's efforts are strongest when our efforts are useless."

NEW PERSPECTIVE ON KINGDOM-MINDED THINGS

A true starting point begins with where you are standing and the lens you are looking through. Our perception is the greatest key to influencing our lives. Let's seek proper perspective first, and through growth, a fulfilled life of hope and healing will follow.

At times, life can feel like a maze. There are many emotional and psychological benefits to the problem-solving processes. A maze is a task where we have to make decisions about what to do at certain points to continue toward a final goal.

This activity is a great way to practice setting out to achieve something that may appear challenging at first.

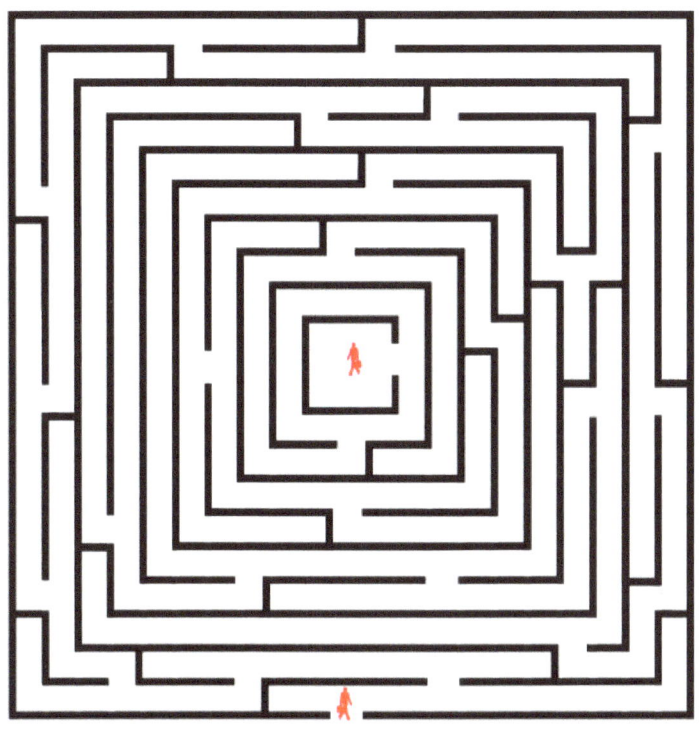

Week 8: Guilt Has Had Us Long Enough

APPLYING THIS PRINCIPLE THROUGH PRAYER

Father, please grant me revelation - revelation of my mind and spirit. I know that you sent your personal best in Your Son, Jesus, so I would no longer have to be burdened with the mistakes I have made on my Journey. Because of His sacrifice, I am no longer burdened with the pain of the damage I have inflicted on others. Please touch their hearts and let them hear my cry of apology. Most of all, Father, remind me each day that Jesus paid it all, and all to Him I owe! In Jesus' name, Amen.

Stephen Scoggins

WRITE YOUR PRAYER

At times, we can take responsibility, seek restitution, and ask for forgiveness, but the other party may not be in a place to extend grace. This is where we must release our guilt and reach out to God Almighty to speak to this person on our behalf. One of the greatest gifts God continues to give us is His Grace. Write a prayer of praise for the grace that God bestowed upon us. Reflect on how you will both share and accept grace into your life, not only with others, but for yourself as well.

_____

_____

_____

_____

_____

_____

DRAW YOUR JOURNEY

You have been doing a lot of reflecting this week through your words and His Word. This page is your canvas to exercise the creative gifts He has given you. Use this page to illustrate this week's thought and prompt to gain the clarity needed to see your Journey from a different perspective.

Week 8: Guilt Has Had Us Long Enough

From our study of scripture this week, we know that God forgives our trespasses through grace. How does this change your environment and God's world? When we are shown grace, it moves beyond ourselves and becomes a shared experience. It strengthens and grows all those involved, both individually and collectively. Divide this page in half, split right across the middle. On the bottom, draw a moment of grace you have been shown. On the top, draw a picture of your community impacted by grace. By doing so, when you are overcome by guilt, you will be able to access this picture and make grace a reality.

Week 8: Guilt Has Had Us Long Enough

BUILDING PRINCIPLES

Congratulations!

You are well on your way to healing, understanding, and building a stronger relationship with God the Father.

Every step you take on your Journey, you are tearing down the walls that stand in your way. As you take these walls apart, use the blocks to build your foundation for success. This will be your guide as you intentionally shape the foundation for your success.

WEEK 8 BUILDING PRINCIPLE: FREEDOM IN GRACE

To feel guilt is to be human. It is your conscious speaking through your heart. However, we are not meant to carry this burden with us all throughout our Journey. Review your revelations this week and how they have led you to the grace of God. Through practice, we are able to overcome guilt, make things right, and build our relationship with God Almighty.

_____

_____

_____

_____

_____

_____

_____

_____

But by the grace of God I am what I am, and his grace toward me was not in vain. On the contrary, I worked harder than any of them, though it was not I, but the grace of God that is with me.

1 Corinthians 15:10, ESV

Week 9

Operate in Discernment, Not Deception

Then we will no longer be infants, tossed back and forth by the waves, and blown here and there by every wind of teaching and by the cunning and craftiness of people in their deceitful scheming. Instead, speaking the truth in love, we will grow to become in every respect the mature body of him who is the head, that is, Christ.

Ephesians 4:14-15, NIV

God's Truth sets us FREE!

Obstacle: Deception
Building Principle: Wisdom

We can break the pattern of deception around us and build a legacy of honesty.

Regardless of your family history or habits, you can speak the truth and gain wisdom through your relationship with Him. If you have not come to this conclusion already, God is not someone who says something without backing it up. He showed us His love by sending His only beloved Son down to Earth in the form of a man. He could have chosen any form! Yet He chose to send Jesus down to us as a baby, left to the protection of Mary and Joseph until He was crucified on the cross to wipe away our sins.

He suffered human weakness, thirst, wounds, and (perhaps most relatable of all) temptation. Remember when Satan tempted Jesus in the desert, asking Him to prove God's greatness? The tool Satan uses hand-in-hand with temptation is deception. We do not always have the stamina and steadfast faith of Jesus, but we learn from the times we fall.

I was married to a woman that I truly and deeply loved. I believed I could mend the parts of her that were broken by a tumultuous past. I gave my marriage everything that I could possibly give, praying for clarity or (if it was His will) to move away from the relationship.

Together, my then-wife and I went through six years of counseling, but she never put forth the effort I hoped to see her make to save our marriage. I was fairly certain she had been unfaithful to me, but I went through many years of doubt before she confessed. This was very hard to wrestle with. In my heart, I forgave her, but it was hard for me to move forward. I came to know that not only did she deceive me, but I deceived myself.

I wanted to step into the savior role for her, where in reality, only He could take on this role for her. Through the grace of God, I was able to overcome this deception and allow God to bless me with fruitful relationships, friendships, and areas where I am valued because I know my Father in Heaven loves me as much as He loved His own beloved Son.

I am not saying that I want us to live in deception. What we need to understand is that as each deception comes to light, we gain the wisdom and discernment to be able to avoid Satan's traps in the future.

Just as we learn a new language or learn to ride a bike, we can only hone a skill by practicing. In this activity, you will practice identifying deception. These questions will prompt you through memories, the feelings they trigger, and what your actions were. Your study here will help you determine when you are being deceived and encourage you to stay the path.

Finish the following sentence: I feel manipulated when I hear...

_____

_____

What was the consequence of a time when you ignored advice?

_____

_____

Am I deceiving others in my life? What do I consider a "white lie?"

_____

_____

What would my life look like if I were completely transparent?

_____

_____

How do I decide who to trust?

_____

_____

MIRROR, MIRROR...

For our next activity, we will remain on the same train of thought, but we will need one additional tool. Take this book and go somewhere you have access to a mirror, preferably somewhere you can talk to yourself and make funny faces without anyone passing judgment. We are about to exercise your brain in knowing when you are being deceived or manipulated and when you are being told the truth.

All right, now that you're here, this is what I'm asking of you. You will be testing yourself and emulating corresponding positive or negative expressions. At first, this may be stiff and awkward. However, this activity will show you the importance of positive self-talk through recognizing the emotions the words prompt.

Here we go!

Say something negative about yourself, and then make a disgusted face (as if you smelled something rotten) at yourself in the mirror.

Below, jot down what you said to yourself and how it made you feel.

_____

_____

Next!

Say something positive about yourself, and then smile (like you won the lottery) at yourself. Look at those pretty pearly whites!

Below, jot down what you said to yourself and how it made you feel.

_____

_____

It is proven that your brain reacts to the emotions/faces you make. By linking the words to your expression and emotion in your brain, you are making valuable connections.

CHANGING THE MEANING

For the following words, write a definition that reflects how each word can make you stronger and help you on your Journey.

The Journey Principles talks about using adversity as a tool to build a better life. Here is your chance to practice and help change your relationships with these words. It will also help you to worship God with a learning heart. By changing these words from a negative to a positive point of view, you will change your relationship with them and build a new story around them. The importance is to build GRATITUDE for how they will sustain you.

Deceive

_____

_____

_____

Temptation

_____

_____

_____

Mislead

_____

_____

_____

TRUST

Trust is putting faith into action. When we trust a person, we are willing to rely on them to do something and not worry about it. The more we feel sure about someone, the more we are willing to trust them. Building a trusting relationship with God starts with prayer. I want to share these foundations for building trust that I have learned through personal experience.

T.R.U.S.T.

Take action:
It's not a bet if there's no money. It's not trust if there's no action. We build trust through repeated action and consistent character. The first go is a trial, the second is a redo, but trust is established by demonstrating consistency over time.

How do you build foundations for trust in your relationships?

_____

What attributes make someone trustworthy? How do you see this in yourself?

_____

Release what you can't control:
If you're still worried about an uncontrollable situation, you are still struggling to trust.
Holding onto things we can't control is like shouting at the TV screen to help your team win. It seems to help, but really, the only person it affects is YOU.

On your Journey, what burden are you carrying that you could release?

_____

How can you balance some responsibility and release the rest?

_____

Unarm your defenses:
Nothing worth having comes easily. Trust involves personal risk. It may hurt if others fail you, but if you don't trust others, your life will be limited to what you can do alone.

In what ways are you defensive or unwilling to trust people?

_____

Instead of control, how can you extend grace to those you trust?

_____

Week 9: Operate in Discernment, Not Deception

Serve others:
By helping others, you practice being on the receiving end of trust and you build your own trustworthiness.

How have you developed a trustworthy character?

_____

Who relies on you? What do they rely on you for?

_____

Talk to a supportive friend:
We draw energy and support from human connection and community. We may be extroverts or introverts, but God designed all of us to commune with one another.

Trusting a person with our feelings, scars, and secrets can be uncomfortable. By human nature, we are cautious about who we disclose sensitive information to. However, it is through trust that we begin to share our burdens with others and lighten the load.

Who are the people in your life who give you energy?

_____

Journey Principle 9:
"Operate in Discernment, Not Deception"

Read the story of Jacob in Genesis 32:1-33:20. Throughout this workbook, I will ask you to look at Jacob's story and find areas in your life where you may have experienced similar emotions or concerns. Take the time to sit back and reflect on those times.

EL-ELOHE-ISRAEL

So Esau said, "Let me leave with you some of the people who are with me." But he said, "What need is there? Let me find favor in the sight of my lord."

So Esau returned that day on his way to Seir. But Jacob journeyed to Succoth, and built himself a house and made booths for his livestock. Therefore the name of the place is called Succoth. And Jacob came safely to the city of Shechem, which is in the land of Canaan, on his way from Paddan-aram, and he camped before the city.

And from the sons of Hamor, Shechem's father, he bought for a hundred pieces of money the piece of land on which he had pitched his tent. There he erected an altar and called it El-Elohe-Israel.

Genesis 33: 15-20, ESV

As our story of Jacob draws to a close, we see how Jacob dedicates his life to the Lord. Recall a time when you have praised God's name, even if it was as early as our first week together. How did this change your heart and your days? Remember this moment and pray to Him when you feel yourself struggling and drifting.

This week, we are learning how the evil one uses deception to turn our eyes away from our Heavenly Father. Through prayer and discernment, we will be strong enough to withstand deception. Jacob's model of steadfast faith in the Lord inspires us to stay true to Him. This week, find one person with whom you can share the lessons you have learned over our past eight weeks together. Pour your heart out to God and let Him know you are grateful.

THE GILBEONITE DECEPTION

Joshua 9: 1-27, NIV

Now when all the kings west of the Jordan heard about these things – the kings in the hill country, in the western foothills, and along the entire coast of the Mediterranean Sea as far as Lebanon (the kings of the Hittites, Amorites, Canaanites, Perizzites, Hivites and Jebusites) – they came together to wage war against Joshua and Israel.

However, when the people of Gibeon heard what Joshua had done to Jericho and Ai, they resorted to a ruse: They went as a delegation whose donkeys were loaded with worn-out sacks and old wineskins, cracked and mended. They put worn and patched sandals on their feet and wore old clothes. All the bread of their food supply was dry and moldy. Then they went to Joshua in the camp at Gilgal and said to him and the Israelites, "We have come from a distant country; make a treaty with us."

The Israelites said to the Hivites, "But perhaps you live near us, so how can we make a treaty with you?"

"We are your servants," they said to Joshua.

But Joshua asked, "Who are you and where do you come from?"

They answered: "Your servants have come from a very distant country because of the fame of the Lord your God. For we have heard reports of him: all that he did in Egypt, and all that he did to the two kings of the Amorites east of the Jordan – Sihon king of Heshbon, and Og king of Bashan, who reigned in Ashtaroth. And our elders and all those living in our country said to us, 'Take provisions for your journey; go and meet them and say to them, "We are your servants; make a treaty with us."' This bread of ours was warm when we packed it at home on the day we left to come to you. But now see how dry and moldy it is. And these wineskins that we filled were new, but see how cracked they are. And our clothes and sandals are worn out by the very long journey." The Israelites sampled their provisions but did not inquire of the Lord. Then Joshua made a treaty of peace with them to let them live, and the leaders of the assembly ratified it by oath.

Three days after they made the treaty with the Gibeonites, the Israelites heard that they were neighbors, living near them. So the Israelites set out and on the third day came to their cities: Gibeon, Kephirah, Beeroth and Kiriath Jearim. But the Israelites did not attack them, because the leaders of the assembly had sworn an oath to them by the Lord, the God of Israel.

The whole assembly grumbled against the leaders, but all the leaders answered, "We have given them our oath by the Lord, the God of Israel, and we cannot touch them now. This is what we will do to them: We will let them live, so that God's wrath will not fall on us for breaking the oath we swore to them."

They continued, "Let them live, but let them be woodcutters and water carriers in the service of the whole assembly." So the leaders' promise to them was kept.

Then Joshua summoned the Gibeonites and said, "Why did you deceive us by saying, 'We live a long way from you,' while actually you live near us? You are now under a curse: You will never be released from service as woodcutters and water carriers for the house of my God."

They answered Joshua, "Your servants were clearly told how the Lord your God had commanded his servant Moses to give you the whole land and to wipe out all its inhabitants from before you. So we feared for our lives because of you, and that is why we did this. We are now in your hands. Do to us whatever seems good and right to you."

So Joshua saved them from the Israelites, and they did not kill them. That day he made the Gibeonites woodcutters and water carriers for the assembly, to provide for the needs of the altar of the Lord at the place the Lord would choose. And that is what they are to this day.

GOLDEN NUGGETS
Lessons from Joshua

Reflect on the Gibeonites' story of deception. Below are three questions that are designed to engage your mind and heart. Write your personal inspired belief about what the passage is saying and how it is relevant to building awesome relationships.

Our relationship with God is strengthened when we know how to build support around us and use others to help us on our walk with God. For this reflection, use quotes from famous literary authors to make the connection between Biblical stories and your life.

Write the connection you feel with the quote below, whether it is to your Journey or a Biblical passage.

"A lie that is half-truth is the darkest of all lies."

Alfred Tennyson

_____

_____

"Oh, what a tangled web we weave...when first we practice to deceive."

Walter Scott, Marmion

_____

_____

"The truest way to be deceived is to think oneself more knowing than others."

François de La Rochefoucauld, Francois de La Rochefoucauld's Book

_____

_____

SEARCHING THE SCRIPTURE FROM WITHIN

Now is the time to take God's Word into your hands and search for the passages that will guide you through your Journey and strengthen your prayer. In the paragraphs that follow, let His Word flow through you and speak to your Journey. By taking the time to review and record His holy Word, you will grow a greater awareness of His awesome power in your life.

1. Often times, when we think of deception, we either think of how we are deceiving others or how others are deceiving us. While this holds different amounts of truth for different people, consider how we deceive ourselves. God wishes us to have wisdom while Satan will attack us with weapons of lies and half-truths disguised as prophesy. Discover scripture where God urges us to act in truth and refer back to it when those half-truths and lies begin to lead you astray.

Scripture:

_____

_____

Week 9: Operate in Discernment, Not Deception

2. When facing someone or something that lies to us and diverts us, it is difficult to determine what is true. Just as we face the temptation Satan places in our paths, so too did Jesus. Refer to Matthew 4: 1-11. How can Jesus' wisdom in these trials apply to those you are facing?

Scripture:

_____

_____

3. Without wisdom, we will stumble through the darkness. God will guide our way when we ask for the wisdom to move forward and the understanding to know the difference between His truth and Satan's lies. Find a verse in scripture that will inspire your prayer for wisdom.

Scripture:

_____

_____

4. We are told that wisdom will be the tool to fight deception. Search and record Scripture that tell us how we benefit from wisdom. When facing deception, know that by using the wisdom given to you by God Almighty, you will come out of the situation stronger.

Scripture:

_____

_____

QUESTIONS TO MOVE YOU FORWARD
WRITE YOUR ANSWERS ON THE LINES BELOW THE QUESTIONS.

God gave us the gift of choice. Learning to ask yourself the right questions is something you have to practice. When we begin to develop this skill, that is when we can truly move forward in both our relationship with Him and in taking the next steps on our Journey.

Name three trials of deception you have faced, past or present. How can you use the lessons gleaned from these situations for future trials?

1. _____

2. _____

3. _____

Name one half-truth or falsehood you have been telling yourself. How will you free yourself from the deception Satan has tried to lure you into this week?

_____

_____

Do you know of someone living in deception? How will you use God's Word to bring them back to the truth this week?

_____

_____

Think of a time when you were deceived. How did you come to know that you were not told the truth or the whole truth? Write a few sentences on how you can use this gained wisdom to avoid similar obstacles in the future.

_____

_____

_____

SETTING YOUR PATH FOR GROWTH

"Nothing is impossible, the word itself says I'm possible."

Audrey Hepburn

During these ten weeks and after, make sure that these goals are for YOU! Pray to God for guidance when you set your goals to match the path He has carved out for you.

There are so many excuses for not moving forward. A lot of the time, the reasons why we fail to accomplish our goals is because we lie to ourselves. "I am not enough," "I just can't do what they can," or "I don't have the right tools." Do you see what the common factor here is? It's YOU. The beautiful part about this is that YOU can change.

I want you to consider a goal that you may have struggled with in the past or find yourself struggling with now. What is your mindset around this goal?

_____

_____

_____

Take this mindset and flip it 180 degrees. How can you bring a positive attitude and thought process toward this goal? How will you intentionally change your approach to this goal?

_____

_____

_____

Hold onto this new perspective as you continue through the week and then come back to this page. Jot your notes of the difference it made here:

_____

_____

_____

APPLYING THIS PRINCIPLE THROUGH PRAYER

Father, thank You so much for seeking me out and helping me to grow and mature. Please guide me in my purpose, plan, and help me to discern what is of You and what is not. Please lead me not unto temptation, but deliver me from evil. Lead me to green pastures and guide my path into Your light. Help me to use my name in Jabez's place and trust you as you guide my mind and heart. In Jesus' name, Amen.

Stephen Scoggins

WRITE YOUR PRAYER

We all know that we do not wish to be deceived or trapped by falsehoods. These are the tools Satan uses on us all too often. Do not be discouraged by this! God gives us the gift of discernment and wisdom through His Word and through the Spirit to consciously confront Satan's tactics. Write a prayer to God to grant you with the wisdom to recognize when Satan is playing his wicked games. Through His Holy understanding, you will learn to find the wolf among the sheep.

_____

_____

_____

_____

_____

_____

DRAW YOUR JOURNEY

You have been doing a lot of reflecting this week through your words and His Word. This page is your canvas to exercise the creative gifts He has given you. Use this page to illustrate this week's thought and prompt to gain the clarity needed to see your Journey from a different perspective.

What deceptions or half-truths are you facing, past or present? Visualize what these look like in your life and draw two or three of them here. This week, you are drawing your interpretation of the phrase, "Satan will disguise himself as a wolf in sheep's clothing." Above each deception, write what the Truth is. (i.e. If you are deceiving yourself into believing that you are a failure, write that you are a student and learning from your mistakes.)

Week 9: Operate in Discernment, Not Deception

BUILDING PRINCIPLES

Congratulations!

You are well on your way to healing, understanding, and building a stronger relationship with God the Father.

Every step you take on your Journey, you are tearing down the walls that stand in your way. As you take these walls apart, use the blocks to build your foundation for success. This will be your guide as you intentionally shape the foundation for your success.

WEEK 9 BUILDING PRINCIPLE: WISDOM

Deception is a tricky thing, isn't it? It is sly, sneaky, and we are often ensnared in Satan's trap before we realize what has happened. Yet we are blessed because God knows of Satan's tricks! What knowledge have you gained from Week 9? Have you found a deception that you have been struggling with, whether it is external or internal? How has He revealed wisdom to you this week? Detail your knowledge here to refer back to when you feel your life is being influenced by an untruth.

_____

_____

_____

_____

_____

_____

_____

_____

If any of you lacks wisdom, you should ask God, who gives generously to all without finding fault, and it will be given to you.

James 1:5, NIV

Week 10

This Too Shall Pass and What Comes Next Will Be Greater

Let us not become weary in doing good, for at the proper time we will reap a harvest if we do not give up.

Galatians 6:9, NIV

Find HOPE in your struggle. God is not done.

**Obstacle: Discouragement
Building Principle: Perseverance**

Have you ever gone on a long hike or climbed up a hill or even summited a mountain of over 14,000 feet high? Take a moment to remember what that experience was like for you. Do you remember the sweat you shed and the wildflowers you saw on your way up? Did you take a moment at the top to appreciate all the work that went into reaching this peak? Or did you reach your goal and say to yourself: "Okay, this is nice, let's go back down."?

Which of those questions gives you more satisfaction? More than likely, your answer is all but the last question! This is because the hike or climb was all about the experience of reaching the goal. You rejoiced because you persevered, and you never gave up.

Life's Journey is about who you become, who you inspire, and how you give.

Life's Journey is about how we get back to the One with whom we were separated from due to the sin of the world.

I have found that God the Father will give you all the inspiration and wisdom you will ever need. His Wisdom is always taught when we least expect it. When we understand the purpose behind the pain, our struggles begin to resemble new life.

Don't be discouraged and never ever quit loving, no matter how much pain you experience! The pain and suffering you go through prepares you for the person you are meant to be. Our day-to-day struggles often seem like more than we can handle, but when you're overwhelmed, know that God is there next to you.

As you know from my story, I have faced devastating depression in my life, to the point where I found myself sitting on an overpass, ready to end it all. I made a few phone calls to my loved ones but wasn't able to reach anyone. Then, Mamawama answered the phone and saved my life.

Mamawama, Susan Batts, was the mother of Ashley, a girl I dated in high school. Ashley was the first girlfriend that had taken my heart by storm and I was Ashley's first boyfriend altogether. Even when the relationship ended, Susan always treated me like a son and took care of me as her own.

On the bridge that day, she knew something was wrong, she could hear it in my voice. Just before I hung up, I heard these words: "This too shall pass and what comes next will be greater." These words reverberated through me and my love for Susan would not let her down.

I am blessed with a permanent reminder of Mamawama in the palm of my left hand. Now, when I feel down, I can look at my my lightning bolt scar in my left hand and remember her love and wisdom.

You see, one afternoon, Ashley and I went to my trailer, but I forgot my keys and we were locked out. I tried so hard to open a window that it broke, cutting my hand and I was bleeding badly.

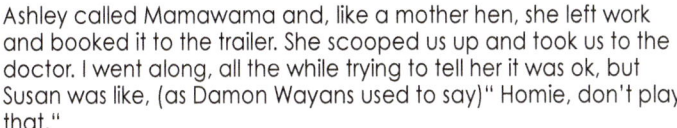

Ashley called Mamawama and, like a mother hen, she left work and booked it to the trailer. She scooped us up and took us to the doctor. I went along, all the while trying to tell her it was ok, but Susan was like, (as Damon Wayans used to say)" Homie, don't play that."

We sat there as I was getting stitched up, my father in one corner crying and Mamawama tearfully watching them repair my hand. Without a word, she paid the medical expenses, knowing full well that we did not have the money to repay her. But she did it anyway. As we left, I told her I would, in fact, pay her back. She giggled and said not to worry about that, my hand was more important.

Do you have a reminder of someone who loves and inspires you? Even if you don't have a physical reminder, know that He created everything around you and you are His greatest creation, conceived in love. What does your reminder look like and how does it help you? Look to this reminder in times of struggle and know that you are loved.

_____

_____

I am so blessed to have had this woman in my life. She gave me the guidance that only a mother can give to her child. Little did she know that she would be my saving grace and my inspiration to help others.

THE POWER OF GRIEVING

I loved my Nanny so much. I felt hurt and lost without her, but I also knew that she was home in Heaven with the Heavenly Father.

My brothers and sisters in Christ, grief is real, but so is healing. Every sorrow and season of grief we walk through is meant to teach us something or guide us along our Journey.

Nanny taught me to make mac 'n' cheese, get ready for school, and take care of my brother. We were blessed with her compassion. These gifts she gave freely remind me of how she brought our family back together.

PROCESSING GRIEF

Recall how Elisabeth Kübler-Ross describes the stages of grief:

1. **Denial:** The disbelief that this is happening.
2. **Anger:** Trying to figure out why it is happening.
3. **Bargaining:** If someone can just make this go away, I will do or give...
4. **Depression:** The pain is too much to bear.
5. **Acceptance:** You have finally found peace.

Have you come across these stages of sorrow before? They are by no means concrete. We all go through sorrow in different ways and experience the phases at our own pace.

In the following questions, we will be revisiting a time when you have experienced a great loss in your life. I will help you look at this from a new perspective and I hope to help you find God's purpose for this loss.

I am thankful that you are allowing me to walk through this time of loss with you. After we go through these questions, you may still be hurting from remembering this loss. Look forward to the time you spend in Scripture; let His Word heal the pain and sorrow in your life.

Select one hurt or loss, and evaluate where you stand in the "5 Stages of Grief" for that experience. Which stage do you find yourself coming back to?

_____

I had my uncle and family around when Nanny died. Who in your life has walked through periods of grief with you?

_____

In your life, who is facing sorrow or grief and how can you show them support and compassion?

_____

_____

_____

CHANGING THE MEANING

For the following words, write a definition that reflects how each word can make you stronger and help you on your Journey.

The Journey Principles talks about using adversity as a tool to build a better life. Here is your chance to practice and help change your relationships with these words. It will also help you to worship God with a learning heart. By changing these words from a negative to a positive point of view, you will change your relationship with them and build a new story around them. The importance is to build GRATITUDE for how they will sustain you.

Overwhelmed

_____

_____

_____

Overpowered

_____
_____
_____

Struggle

_____
_____
_____

Journey Principle 10:
"This Too Shall Pass and What Comes Next Will Be Greater"

> **THE LORD'S PRAYER**
>
> Our Father in heaven, hallowed be your name. Your Kingdom come, your will be done, on earth as in heaven. Give us today our daily bread. Forgive us our sins, as we forgive those who sin against us. Lead us not into temptation, but deliver us from evil. For the kingdom, the power and the glory are yours. Now and forever. Amen

"You may encounter many defeats, but you must not be defeated. In fact, it may be necessary to encounter defeats, so you can know who you are, what you can rise from, how you can still come out of it."

Maya Angelou

Read the above quote by Maya Angelou and reflect on the lessons you learned over the past weeks and how much you have grown in your walk with God.

Now add to your prayer skill by writing a prayer of gratitude for the past weeks' lessons.

_____

_____

_____

_____

_____

_____

_____

_____

_____

_____

_____

_____

_____

SEARCHING THE SCRIPTURE FROM WITHIN

Now is the time to take God's Word into your hands and search for the passages that will guide you through your Journey and strengthen your prayer. In the paragraphs that follow, let His Word flow through you and speak to your Journey. By taking the time to review and record His holy Word, you will grow a greater awareness of His awesome power in your life.

1. Uncover a passage where God has displayed His plans for you. How can you find peace in knowing that every obstacle you face and every season of discouragement is a stepping stone to His glory? The scripture you find will bring you perseverance in the presence of doubt and fear.

Scripture:

_____

_____

2. Look for a passage of peace and hope to be reminded of when you are feeling overwhelmed by the weight of life. When you read these words, the Holy Spirit will fill you to the brim so that the discouragement is washed away by His promise and plans for you, His child.

Scripture:

_____

_____

3. How is the Lord bringing joy into your life this week? Search for scripture that gives you a spark of joy in knowing that He is with you even when you stumble and fall, and that He is with you always.

Scripture:

_____

_____

4. How is the Lord pouring peace into your heart as you take on the tasks of the week? This scripture will bring stillness where restlessness once stirred. May these words bring you to a place where you feel calm and strengthened to take the steps He has planned for your Journey.

Scripture:

_____

_____

QUESTIONS TO MOVE YOU FORWARD
WRITE YOUR ANSWERS ON THE LINES BELOW THE QUESTIONS.

God gave us the gift of choice. Learning to ask yourself the right questions is something you have to practice. When we begin to develop this skill, that is when we can truly move forward in both our relationship with Him and in taking the next steps on our Journey.

Identify three things or events you are looking forward to in the future, near or far. Remember, what comes next will be greater!

1. _____

2. _____

3. _____

What is one step you can take to manage your feelings of being overwhelmed?

_____

_____

Who will you reach out to this week to thank them for their support?

_____

_____

Write a brief prayer to God to ask for help. Though we feel we can handle everything on our own sometimes, God is always with us to help carry the weight of our burdens and guide us along the way. He is our partner in grief and in joy.

_____

_____

_____

SETTING YOUR PATH FOR GROWTH

"Don't follow the crowd, let the crowd follow you."

Margaret Thatcher

During these ten weeks and after, make sure that these goals are for YOU! Pray to God for guidance when you set your goals to match the path He has carved out for you.

We are nearly at the end of week ten and this signifies our last goal meeting. Before we get started, I want to say how very proud I am of you! Ten weeks is a good chunk of time to commit yourself to and you have come a long way. I want you to take a moment and reflect on how far you have come. Write five steps you have taken toward accomplishing your goal and what you have learned:

_____

_____

_____

_____

_____

For our final goal setting, write how you will continue to set goals for the future and how you will hold yourself accountable. Whether you connect with a Master Mind group through The Journey Principles Institute or call up a good friend once a week, having an accountability partner will keep you on the right path. By staying on the path, you will be accomplishing everything you set out to do.

I will keep myself accountable by ...

_____

_____

_____

ACTIONS STEPS FOR PERSEVERANCE

I have studied the success of others and have found that there is a pattern for perseverance. Follow the five steps below to feed the fire of your perseverance. When you stumble, take the time to stand tall, adjust your focus, and keep going. Let the words that follow inspire you to continue your Journey.

1. Engaging the moment – Living a life of perseverance is not simply saying, "C'est la vie." It is not a mere acceptance of circumstance, but the application of experience. You should use your life lessons to help shape your ideology, morals, ethics, and how you take action in the world. Accepting the lessons of the past helps to overcome the fear of failure and allows you to concentrate on the here and now. While you should use this wisdom to experience the present, trusting in perseverance will also allow you to overcome the unpredictable roads ahead.

From a faith perspective, I think it's important to remember how precious our time one earth is. James 4:14 says, "Why, you do not even know what will happen tomorrow. What is your life? You are a mist that appears for a little while and then vanishes." Honor the Father by living life fully. Don't look back with regret and wonder what more you could have done to advance His Kingdom.

2. Accepting change – C.S. Lewis is quoted as saying "to be in time, means to change." Change is a part of life. It is inevitable. From what I have observed of those who seem to exhibit strength in perseverance, it almost seems like change is welcomed. Maybe they just have a better understanding that growth accompanies change. Maybe, from their point-of-view, living a life without challenges isn't living at all. Whatever the reason, the people that I consider to be mentally tough are also the ones who are the most willing to step out of their comfort zones. Coincidence? Absolutely not.

For the believer, I think that one of the first steps to accepting Christ is admitting that you are broken and missing a piece of yourself without the King of Kings. Without that recognition, there would be no desire to change. Don't ever let that process become stagnant. Don't ever shy away from letting God stretch and teach you. As you grow closer to Him, trusting more and fearing less, earnestly seek the ways that He would call you onward and upward.

3. Take responsibility – John Burroughs said, "A man can fail many times, but he isn't a failure until he begins to blame somebody else." Wow! I don't need to add much more to that. Persevering means taking responsibility for your failures. Don't shift the blame to

others, but look for the ways in which you could have done better. Learn and grow, but at the same time learn to recognize when things are outside of your control and don't beat yourself up over the things that you cannot change.

4. Learn from your mistakes – I believe the quote that "Insanity is doing the same thing over and over and expecting different results," is attributed to Albert Einstein. While that's obviously not the technical definition of insanity, the quote does ring with some truth. I think we all have a friend or acquaintance that just seems to keep screwing up in the same ways time and time again. That's the exact opposite of perseverance! Persevering isn't just pushing forward; it's moving forward with accumulated and calculated wisdom. It's digging through the trash of past mistakes and developing the treasure for your future!

5. Never give up – Okay, so this is kind of an obvious aspect of perseverance, but I grew up in Raleigh, North Carolina where Jim Valvano's "Don't give up...don't ever give up," inspired many long before the V Foundation had the global recognition it has today. I think that it is important to remember that perseverance doesn't just mean pushing forward after failure. Perseverance also means pushing through the adversity. Be tenacious. Obstacles threaten most successes and the significant achievements in this life are great because of what was overcome to claim triumph. Push forward, keep your head up, and never ever give up.

APPLYING THIS PRINCIPLE THROUGH PRAYER

Father, please cleanse me of any doubts of my self-worth. Please help me to look back and see your fingerprints on the lessons my path has led me to learn. Cleanse me of my stumbling blocks. Show me that failure is never a person, but a lesson to grow from. Help me to know the truth behind "No eye has seen, no ear has heard, and no mind has imagined what God has prepared for those that love Him." (1 Corinthians 2:9, NLT) Lord, in you I am no failure, but only a lump of clay you are molding, and I welcome your design! In Jesus' name, Amen.

Stephen Scoggins

WRITE YOUR PRAYER

Do you find yourself tossing and turning at nights, struggling in the land of "What If?" Are you lost, fighting through the fog of confusion? If you identified with any of this, then you are struggling with the peace that can only be found in God the Father. Develop a prayer designed to grant your life clarity, purpose, and design. Persevere until the blessing is yours! When you make the choice to reach out and connect with the Father, you will feel how much He loves you.

_____

_____

_____

_____

_____

_____

Week 10: This Too Shall Pass and What Comes Next Will Be Great

DRAW YOUR JOURNEY

You have been doing a lot of reflecting this week through your words and His Word. This page is your canvas to exercise the creative gifts He has given you. Use this page to illustrate this week's thought and prompt to gain the clarity needed to see your Journey from a different perspective.

Reach back to a time when you persevered. Now, visualize the largest obstacle you overcame. Draw this obstacle and the tools you used to break it down. Hold this picture in your mind's eye as you go forward in your Journey and know who you are, what you want to achieve, and persist through every obstacle placed in your path. Let this image inspire you to persevere in your Journey and praise His name. For while you are on this earth, it is His will for you to experience the gifts of contentment, joy, and peace.

YOU CAN DO IT

As you have read most of my story by now, you know that I have gone through a season of healing. I traveled many roads, curves, mountains, hills, valleys, and oceans. The Journey is the goal, it is the test, it is the grace, it is the purpose and it will matter to someone! It just may change someone's life when you are willing to fight the battle and persevere.

I hope you can see how we can identify with Jacob in the book of Genesis. We will sometimes act directly in God's will, and other times, directly out of it. It does not matter what that event in life is; it does not take away from what is to come in your life.

I will close with just two thoughts. The first is that as I sat on a cold, curved railing on the bridge and made that phone call to Susan Batts (aka, Mamawama,) I heard the Truth from the Angel in her voice. I learned that Susan had her own Journey. If she had not been brave enough to fight her battle, she would not have been there for mine. You don't know whose life you are meant to save based on the price you are willing to pay.

The second thought is this truth: Death and despair are lies, and life and love are huge truths. What if that call had not been made; what if that call was not answered? There would be no CHE, no book, and no help for the hurting. CHE employs several hundred team members and installation vendors who now share in this vision. People matter, and above that, YOU matter!

I make one request of you: Choose to matter to yourself. Choose to find truth in scripture. Choose to believe the truth of life over the lie of death and know in your heart that the Father loves you so much that He made sure this book ended up in your hands. All He wants is to know you, His son or daughter, His child. He is waiting for you, His Word is waiting for you, and His eternity is waiting for you.

You can do it. You will do it if you just choose to do it!

BUILDING PRINCIPLES

Congratulations!

You are well on your way to healing, understanding, and building a stronger relationship with God the Father.

Every step you take on your Journey, you are tearing down the walls that stand in your way. As you take these walls apart, use the blocks to build your foundation for success. This will be your guide as you intentionally shape the foundation for your success.

WEEK 10 BUILDING PRINCIPLE: PERSEVERANCE

In our final Building Principle, take a moment to acknowledge how far you have come over the ten-week period. What have you achieved? What are you most proud of? How have you grown in your faith? Take this feeling of accomplishment with you as you continue your Journey and look back at this time with a sense of pride.

_____

_____

_____

_____

_____

_____

You turned the final leaf in the workbook but have yet to take the final step in your Journey! Over the past ten weeks, we have walked this path together. Here we are, at our final Principle of the course. Take these ten Principles with you as you continue your Journey. God bless you!

"Give, and it will be given to you. A large quantity, pressed together, shaken down, and running over will be put into your lap because you'll be evaluated by the same standard with which you evaluate others."

Luke 6:38, ISV

ABOUT JOURNEY PRINCIPLES LLC

The "Journey Principles Nation" (JP Nation) is made up of people across the country just like you who have decided to be brave and courageous in applying God's principles to their Journey.

You are familiar with The Journey Principles, and you know who Stephen Scoggins is. Now prepare yourselves to dive into The Journey Principles Institute (JPI). The JPI is a home for you to use the tools you've gained to strengthen relationships with God by applying faith and your life lessons daily. We are here to help others learn how to use the obstacles in their lives – those previously found to be paralyzing – and use them to take the action steps to create success!

The JPI is here to provide you with the community you need to become a leader in Christian Living Counseling and go forth to testify the application of God's principles in your daily life. We also provide continued education for individuals, families, and businesses.

ABOUT THE AUTHORS

Stephen Scoggins

Stephen Scoggins is a successful entrepreneur turned author, minister, speaker and life coach. Founder of three multi-million dollar companies and The Journey Principles Institute, Stephen uses the stories of his life journey to inspire others. From being down-and-out to turning his business into a multi-million dollar venture, he found that his contentment came from his Heavenly Father. Stephen's heart is rooted in his desire to help others on their journeys and ignite their hidden purpose and passion from within.

Stephen now tours internationally, sharing his practical wisdom and techniques with thousands. Through the power of his story and the lessons he has learned, Stephen empowers people through God's principles. The message he shares is how to turn these roadblocks into a foundation for success.

Wendy Muse Greenwood

Wendy Muse's life vision is to help God's people to reach their full potential. She is an accomplished writer, academic, publisher, international training consultant, and co-founder of IFXInsight.

As an award winning program developer, Wendy Muse puts her business acumen and literary art background to work for school districts, universities, community clinics, nonprofits and public safety authorities throughout the US and the UK.

She holds her B.A. in Professional Writing from the University of South Wales where she graduated Summa Cum Laude. Additionally, she holds her LL.M (MA) in Intellectual and Industrial Property Law.

This publication is a personal workbook and is intended exclusively for individual use. This work may not be reproduced for use in a classroom or other group settings or for use by organizations as a part of a training program. Such use may be granted by Journey Principles in written license and upon payment of applicable license fees.

For more information on how to obtain a license, please go to our website:
journeyprinciples.com

Write to:
Journey Principles LLC
423 E. 2nd Street
Clayton, NC 27520

What people are saying

"Stephens's words gave me so much more than hope; they gave me a new sense of courage to break through the pain in my relationship and use it to grow. I read the principles whenever I need a reminder of how to be present and get through the day ahead."

-Amber Muse

"I just finished Stephen's book. I'm going through my own journey, and this book was great. It helped put all my emotions, feelings and thoughts into perspective. Thanks Stephen for sharing your story."

-Chris

"The Journey Principles is a very inspirational autobiographical book written by Stephen Scoggins. Mr. Scoggins draws upon his life experiences to illustrate his guiding principles that lead towards a fulfilling and rewarding life. A must-read!"

-John

"Stephen, your heart actions have been so motivating to me that I am doing things these dates that a few months ago I would never have even considered! I do things even if I am afraid of failure or rejection, and so far ALL of my fears have been for naught and every small step I took out of my comfort zone has a resulted in LEAPS of progress for me and the people I have reached out to and for!!! What a blessing!!"

-Laurie Yaw

"I'm very proud of you and your accomplishments and what you'll continue to do in the future. With Karen by your side, there is nothing you won't be able to do. I think God has brought the two of you together at just the right time. The Navy Seal loss is our big gain...and we are so looking forward to having you in our family...We will continue to support you in any direction you choose to take."

-Mom Salley

What people are saying (Cont'd)

"Demonstrating both vulnerability and insight, Stephen Scoggins uses his personal joys and trials to show the miraculous nature of God's work in his life. In his book The Journey Principles, Scoggins weaves accounts of his past with his insight into topics like spirituality, relationships, and success, creating a unique blend of equal parts memoir and motivation. The Journey Principles is a great resource for those interested in a more spiritual approach to the struggles we all face in life. Because of his unique background, Scoggins tackles difficult topics in an intimate way that feels very accessible to the reader. "

-Madison Carr

"An autobiographical book that's full of inspiration and wisdom, "The Journey Principles" is a great example of turning the tragedies in life into triumphs. Filled with a multitude of examples from his own life, Stephen Scoggins shares his journey as a growing Christian."

-Rebecca Henderson

This book is amazing. What he says is so true and hits home with me. I have to stop reading so I can take the time to absorb what he says and commit it to memory. I have just begun to read this and need to say how much I love this book!

I am a worrier and even through the grief of losing my Mom last month I am hearing his words resound in my mind with such truth from God. Words that will help me defeat my unreal fear and anxiety. I "worried" a lot that my Mom, who was diagnosed with Alzheimer's, would become paranoid in her forgetfulness, maybe mean, and even an invalid lost in her body. But God was merciful, took her home early, and I worried for naught. I want to say 'thank you'! to Stephen for helping me move out of the pit of worry and anxiety and even see God's mercy in my Mom's death. I am humbled and grateful that God loves me and delivered this book to me at just the right time!

-Janet Bledsoe

Stephen Scoggins knocks it out of the park with his tell-all book. The book is an extremely easy read and feels like you are having a conversation with the man himself. After reading, it definitely lit a spark under me and gave me a "why not?" mentality. The stories give you great insight on how combining positivity and faith, you can be anything you want to be. I fully recommend!

-Jake Jablonski

Notes

Notes

www.ingramcontent.com/pod-product-compliance
Lightning Source LLC
Chambersburg PA
CBHW041607220426
43666CB00001B/5